DEAN ALTERMAN

HOW TO BUILD A REAL ESTATE LAW PRACTICE

SECTION OF REAL | TRUST &
PROPERTY | ESTATE LAW

Defending Liberty
Pursuing Justice

Cover design by Tamara Kowalski/ABA Publishing.

ISBN: 978-1-63425-004-7

e-ISBN: 978-1-63425-005-4

Library of Congress Cataloging-in-Publication Data

Alterman, Dean N., author.
 How to build a real estate law practice / by Dean Alterman, Section of Real Property, Trust & Estate Law, American Bar Association.
 pages cm
 Includes bibliographical references and index.
 ISBN 978-1-63425-004-7 (alk. paper)
 1. Real estate lawyers--United States--Handbooks, manuals, etc. 2. Real estate business--Law and legislation--Vocational guidance--United States. 3. Practice of law--United States. I. American Bar Association. Section of Real Property, Trust, and Estate Law, sponsoring body. II. Title.

 KF299.R43A48 2015
 340.068--dc23

Contents

Chapter VII
Staffing Your Office

About the Author

Dean Alterman's varied career includes eight years as a real estate agent and three years as chairman of a county planning commission. Mr. Alterman graduated from Harvard College in 1981 and from Lewis & Clark Law School in 1989. He has practiced real estate and business law in Portland, Oregon since 1989. After working for three other firms (one of which closed its doors forever twelve weeks after he arrived), he opened his own office in 2006, growing it to a four-lawyer firm and then becoming a founding partner of Folawn Alterman & Richardson LLP in 2009, where he now works. He frequently gives presentations and publishes articles on real estate topics. This is his first book.

Chapter I

Why a Real Estate Practice?

You may have already developed a real estate practice and be reading this book for pointers that you can incorporate into your practice and your business plan. If so, congratulations! You've already discovered the rewards and satisfaction that a successful real estate practice will bring. Or perhaps you've already decided to focus your efforts on developing a real estate practice and are reading this book to learn one approach. If so, you already know the advantages that a real estate practice offers to lawyers, and I offer you my best wishes on achieving your goal.

But if you're in your first few years in practice and haven't become known for a particular practice area yet, or if you've just been admitted to the bar, you may be considering several fields in which to focus your efforts. Why choose real estate?

One practical reason to build a real estate practice is that the underlying law changes only slowly. Our colleagues in tax law have to relearn the law every ten or twelve years when Congress overhauls the tax code. Supreme Court decisions and Securities and Exchange Commission (SEC) enforcement actions constantly change the face of securities law. And intellectual property lawyers are constantly encountering new forms of intellectual property for which the law doesn't yet exist.

Unlike tax law and intellectual property, the basic principles of real estate law go back for centuries. The word "mortgage" is more than 700 years old. Bargain and sale deeds go back to the Statute of Uses, which England adopted in 1535. Although the last century has seen new areas develop within real estate (e.g., real estate syndications and land use) or be spun off from real estate law as separate fields (e.g., environmental law), the basic principles of deeds, mortgages, and land titles have stayed about the same. The basic law you learned in school, and that you acquire in your first years of practice, will serve you throughout your career.

Another reason to build a real estate practice is that it's easy to build a base of steady clients. You might write a lease for the owner of a small strip mall. If the owner likes your work, he or she will return when it's time to renew the lease or write a lease for another tenant or sell or finance the building. Also, the owner of the strip mall likely owns other rental real estate that can produce the need for your services and might seek your advice for two or three projects at the same time. A steady real estate client may consult you every year, or more often, possibly even every week. Some of my real estate clients call me three times a week.

By contrast, even the best client of a domestic relations attorney won't require more than one divorce at a time. A "steady client" of a domestic relations practice might be a steady client because of an ongoing child custody dispute but will not have an actual new matter more often than once every five or ten years.

A third reason to focus on real estate is that many projects will teach you something that you can apply later on. Each matter does not stand by itself, and you can learn details about the industry from one project that you can then apply to a project later on. For instance, after you handle several industrial leases, you will have a grasp of what industrial tenants look for that will serve you well if a client who's considering buying a warehouse as an investment asks your opinion. A practice that includes negotiating retail leases will give you a similar understanding of the local retail market. If you work in a part of the country in which lawyers handle residential real estate closings (I don't), you will get to know the local housing market and economy in some depth, and you may become a valued advisor to residential developers and land investors.

The most important reason to choose real estate as your practice area, however, is that you will have fun working with people who are doing imaginative and varied things with real estate. My practice has brought me in contact with auto dealers, office tower developers, the steel industry, and hotels and has given me the opportunity to learn

about beaches, ditches, printing, office leasing, elevators, gasoline sta-
tions, railroads, baseball, steel mills, and foundries. My relationship
with one client gave me the opportunity to become a director of a small
community bank and, later on, its holding company. Another client's
project led me to visit a metals factory in Japan and learn about sinter-
ing oil filters. Three clients have shown me different facets of the steel
industry. I have walked through farms, looked at ditches, climbed on
roofs, slid through crawlspaces, ridden in ancient freight elevators, built
restaurants, refinanced hotels, leased a baseball stadium, and discovered
buried survey markers. Not every day brings something new across my
desk, but every month does.

Some real estate lawyers have found satisfaction in developing an
industry specialty. One lawyer I know was practicing farm law in a small
town when grape growers discovered the surrounding area and started
to buy up his clients' farms. He saw the trend, learned about the special
agricultural and licensing needs of wineries, and soon became the leading expert on wine law in the county. He is always happy to leave his
office and meet with his winery clients at their places of business. Another
lawyer I know became the local expert on the peculiar and confusing
mix of laws that regulate gravel pits. A third lawyer mastered the detail
involved in leasing, building, and financing fast-food restaurants. The
real estate world is full of opportunities for lawyers to have a rewarding
and exciting career.

Within the broad field of real estate law are many specialties, some that
lead to the courtroom and others more suited to a desk in an office. Some
real estate litigators fight for fair compensation for owners of land that the
government wants. Others represent landlords and tenants in eviction suits
ranging from humble trailers to fancy stores. Some office lawyers negotiate leases between national chains and regional shopping centers. Some
help investors buy, finance, and sell apartment buildings. Some draft the
documents that turn apartment buildings into condominiums. A few write
covenants to bind the land for future generations or work to release covenants of yesteryear that have outlived their purpose.

Your work for real estate clients may lead you to learn important elements of tax law and estate planning. Over time you may become a trusted

advisor to several generations of the same family, called on not just to handle specific tasks for the present but to draw on your experience to provide counsel for the future.

Real estate is a wonderful field of law in which to practice. You're going to enjoy it.

Chapter II

Define Your Practice

A. Formulate Your Practice Goal

Now that you have decided to build a real estate practice (or you have decided to stick with tax law, but you like this book so far), you need to define what your practice will be. At this early point, don't define your practice too exactly, but have some idea of what kind of work and what kind of clients you want. Set your practice goal down in writing. It may change—for one thing, the clients you want may not come in the door or may not exist in your marketplace and you may have to change clients or marketplaces—but you need to have at least a starting point.

My starting point 25 years ago was something like this: "I want as clients people who have made a commitment to sustained investment in commercial real estate." Within that sentence I was saying that I was seeking as clients (a) people, rather than impersonal institutions, who (b) had a buy-and-hold, long-term approach to investing (c) in income-producing real estate.

I am not suggesting that my one-sentence description is the best there is. It was the right description for me, at that time, in my market area. It still is. From that sentence, I have built a practice that brings me, on average, one new client every week and one new matter every business day of the year.

Your sentence doesn't need to be my sentence. The important thing is that you have a one- or two-sentence description of what you want your practice to be. Here are some samples of market descriptions that a real estate lawyer might adopt:

- I will be recognized as the local expert in wineries and vineyards.[1]
- I will advise purchasers and sellers of high-end homes.
- I will advise office landlords and tenants.
- I will represent owners' associations in condominiums and subdivisions.
- I will advise property owners and represent them in condemnation actions.
- I will become the expert in property line disputes.

B. Consider Your Market Area: What Real Estate Work Is Available?

Consider your market area when you pick your goal. My friend in winery law is in the middle of Oregon's wine country—his practice area is perfectly suited to his location. He has kept his general agricultural practice, including advising farmers and food processors (where there are farms, there are processors) on federal and state laws and regulations. It wouldn't make sense for him to have the goal to represent landlords and tenants of high-rise office towers: the tallest office building for rent in his town has only six floors, and there isn't enough office leasing there to keep one lawyer busy. By contrast, my city has many office towers, with several dozen different owners, but no vineyards—it wouldn't make sense for me to try to build an agricultural practice here.

If you want to represent buyers and sellers of high-end houses, then you need to be in an area with a lot of high-end homes. If you want to represent owners' associations, then you should be in an area where subdivisions have homeowners' associations. If work that fits with your practice goal doesn't exist in your ZIP Code, then you should change one or the other.

---

1. The friend I wrote about in Chapter I really does enjoy his winery-related law practice immensely.

C. Make Four Groups to Define Your Practice Goals

When you have defined your practice goal in a sentence or two, try the exercise of breaking down legal fields into four groups:

- Work that you want to be known for doing and will actively solicit.
- Work that is outside your primary focus but that you will do if it comes in, whether from current clients or from new clients.
- Work that is outside your primary focus that you will accept from your real estate clients but won't try to take on as single-engagement work from others.
- Work that you do not want and will decline or refer out.

For example, if you adopt the practice goal of "I will advise office and retail landlords and tenants," you might complete this exercise as follows:

- I want to be known for advising office and retail landlords and tenants, negotiating and drafting leases, and handling commercial evictions.
- I am also willing to handle the purchase, sale, exchange, and refinancing of investment real estate for my regular clients and also for others, but I won't actively solicit or market this work to new clients.
- I am willing to handle property tax appeals for my regular clients and to assist with their estate plans, but I will not solicit this work or (usually) take it on as a one-time engagement from someone who is not already my client.
- I will decline or refer out work involving domestic relations, personal injury, and criminal law.

If you've been out of law school for several years, you may already have some real estate clients when you start your own practice. Good! You are starting your new practice with a ready-made group of clients to whom you can market your services. You will be telling your clients that you are defining your practice to focus on real estate, and you will have a chance to define your practice area not just to yourself but also to your existing clients. If your clients think of you as a real estate lawyer, they will be more likely to think of you when a friend asks them to recommend a real estate lawyer. And referral networks can be powerful: the longest referral chain in my practice is from a client A, who referred B, who referred C, who referred D, who referred E, who referred F. Client E referred client F to me 20 years after I first worked for client A.

Your existing clients can also help you define your practice area. Ask them how they view your practice. What real estate situations do they send to you? What real estate work are they sending to other people? Their answers to these questions may give you a sense of how to redefine your real estate practice so that your clients send those matters to you instead of to other lawyers.

Just because you are defining one field to be your practice area does not mean that you must turn down work in other areas. Rather, it means that you are deciding what you wish to become known for doing—what will make your office telephone ring. You are taking the first step toward sending a clear message to the clients you want to have that you are prepared and qualified to work for them.

There may be many types of work in the second and third groups: work that you are willing to do, but that you won't actively develop. For example, your office building owners may have estate planning needs. It makes sense for you to develop the expertise to handle those needs or to develop a good working relationship with a lawyer who does have an active estate planning practice and who doesn't advise clients on real estate matters, rather than to turn this work away altogether. It's a field that is closely linked to your practice area.

The fourth group is the one to be most particular about. Among the many reasons to turn down work in certain practice areas are two very important ones. The first is that you should turn down work in practice areas that you simply don't like to handle. If you take on projects or disputes in fields that you don't enjoy and that aren't related to your main practice area, you're going to put off handling those matters and will develop unhappy clients. The second is that you have an ethical obligation under Rule 1.1 of the Rules of Professional Conduct (RPC) to take on only those matters that you can competently handle. I discuss your ethical obligations to take on only projects that you can competently handle in Chapter X, Section A.

You don't do yourself or your client any favors when you take on a project that you don't know how to handle and where you can't associate with a lawyer who has the skill and expertise to manage it.

D. Provide a Plus Factor When You Learn a Second Practice Area

To provide more value to your real estate clients, you can add a plus factor: Define your practice as real estate with the addition of a practice area, or a specialty, that allows you to provide added value to your clients. You can be more valuable to your real estate clients if you are confident in your knowledge of the tax laws that affect real estate investors, such as the basics of partnership taxation (larger properties are often purchased by limited liability companies that elect to be taxed as partnerships), depreciation, and depreciation recapture on sale. If you handle the purchase and sale of investment property, then you must know the ins and outs of Section 1031 of the Internal Revenue Code, which allows tax-deferred exchanges of investment and business real estate.

You can also study and use a legal field in the second group—the work that is outside your primary focus but that you want to do and will handle if clients bring it to you—as a way to add a plus factor to your primary practice area and differentiate your services from the other real estate lawyers in your community. If you regularly advise clients who are buying and selling land, one way in which you can provide your clients with a plus factor is to become grounded in land use and zoning regulations. In my city, many lawyers practice real estate law, and many practice land use law, but only a few lawyers practice both. Their plates are always full with work from developers who look to them to handle the acquisition of a development site and to obtain the entitlements (permits) from the local government that will allow them to develop the property as they wish. These developers know that they can engage one lawyer to handle both pieces of work and eliminate the chance that their real estate lawyer and their land use lawyer will contradict each other before the government that is to issue the zoning approvals.

E. Identify What Your Practice Does *Not* Include

Identifying the legal fields in the fourth group—the type of work that you won't handle—is easy, but actually turning the work down when existing clients bring it to you is harder. When you define what your practice includes, also determine what your practice will not include, and stick to your determination. For example, you may define your practice goal to become an expert on leasing and selling office buildings and multitenant retail stores. You may also be willing to handle financing, commercial evictions, and other matters that owners of these buildings often have. If this sentence describes your practice goal, you may decide that you will not handle divorces or auto accidents that have no particular relation to your practice area and will require you to work on the schedule of a litigator instead of that of a transactional lawyer.

Personal injury law is not well linked to real estate. People will slip and fall in your clients' office buildings and shopping centers, and your clients' insurance companies will hire lawyers who concentrate on insurance defense to defend them. Even if you are giving your real estate clients sound advice on their obligation to warn invitees and licensees against dangers on their premises and you can recommend corrective measures to take after an accident occurs, your main advice to your clients after someone is injured on their property will be to call their insurance carriers at once. And if you accept plaintiff's personal injury work, you are likely to have a series of one-time clients who don't have any real estate needs and who don't help you build the core of your real estate practice. Put the personal injury work in the fourth group, and leave it to the lawyers who seek it out and know how to handle it.

Put family law disputes (meaning mainly divorces and child custody battles) in the fourth group for two reasons. The first reason is the same as for plaintiff's personal injury work: Except in an unusual circumstance, a divorce client won't become a regular real estate client and won't help you build your real estate practice. The second reason applies to the more ticklish situation in which one of your regular real estate clients expects to be divorced. If you look on one member of the couple as your real estate client but both spouses own the real estate (or it is owned by limited liability companies in which the spouses are both members), then they may believe that you have represented both spouses in the real estate transactions. They may both be current clients under Rule 1.7 of the Rules of Professional Conduct. RPC 1.7(a) prohibits a lawyer, with one exception, from representing a client if the representation involves a "concurrent conflict of interest," defined to include a situation where "the representation of one client will be directly adverse to another client." Your representation of one spouse in his or her divorce will be directly adverse to the other spouse.

The exception to RPC 1.7(a) is in RPC 1.7(b): Even though a concurrent conflict of interest exists, a lawyer may represent the client if (in the rule's words):

1. the lawyer reasonably believes that the lawyer will be able to provide competent and diligent representation to each affected client;
2. the representation is not prohibited by law;
3. the representation does not involve the assertion of a claim by one client against another client represented by the lawyer in the same litigation or other proceeding before a tribunal; and
4. each affected client gives informed consent, confirmed in writing.

You can reasonably believe that you could represent both spouses on a matter in which they have a common interest, such as evicting a nonpaying tenant from their property, but you cannot reasonably believe that you could provide competent and diligent representation to one spouse in the divorce itself, including seeking to obtain as large a share of the marital property as possible from the other spouse while you are concurrently representing and being paid by the other spouse for some other project. Leave your clients' divorces to the experts.

F. Define Your Practice by Industry Instead of by Legal Topic

As an alternative to defining your practice by a legal topic, you can define your practice by an industry. Consider defining your practice to be how clients might see their problems, rather than to fit neatly within the categories you learned while in school. For example, a lawyer who defines her practice area simply as "tax" and markets her practice that way may find that she gets calls not only from people with income tax problems and disputes with the Internal Revenue Service (the sort of work she is hoping for) but also people who want to challenge their property tax assessments, who are in arguments with local government over business taxes and licenses, and who wish to protest against the tax system generally. She might define the practice that she actually wants to have as follows: "I advise and represent people and businesses who want to manage their tax liabilities, whether in everyday operations or in buying and selling real estate, or in transferring wealth to the next generation." That description includes income tax, business organization, and estate planning. Yet it also describes a specific group of prospective clients.

A real estate lawyer who wants to focus on a particular industry might define the practice as follows: "I represent and advise owners of hotels when they want to buy, sell, lease, or finance their investments, or deal with their franchisor." That advice might include real estate, income tax, property tax, land use, franchise agreements, and commercial lending. This focused description covers several fields of law. It also communicates to the target group of prospective clients exactly who they are. Prospective clients, even some sophisticated ones, may not know exactly what type of legal problem they have, but they always know what industry they are in.

G. Be Wary of Starting a One-Client Practice

You may be practicing with a firm where you have one large-client relationship that occupies most or all of your workday. Be cautious when you think about starting an independent practice that you do not rely on the work of that one client following you to your own shop. There is the obvious risk that no matter how much that client raves about the quality of your work, the account may not follow you to your independent practice. It may turn out that although your contact at the client company (especially if it's a corporate client) is enthusiastic about your work, someone else at the client company—whom you don't know—actually controls the relationships with outside counsel. It may also be the case that your client has relationships with other people at your firm, and large parts of the work that you hope will follow you will instead stay with your former colleagues who have been handling those matters for the client.

It also may turn out that the client does follow you to your own office and sends you enough work to keep you as busy as you want to be right up until the day that you handle the sale of the client's properties as the client retires from business. At that point, the client has no more legal work to send to you. Or the client's nephew graduates from law school, or one of the client's other advisors doesn't like you, or . . . , and then you go from having one client to having zero clients.

The problem with having a practice that depends entirely or mostly on one client is similar to the problem of owning a single-tenant building: the building's vacancy rate is either 0 percent or 100 percent. Your practice will be much more stable if you have ten clients who send you $25,000/year of work each than if you have one client who sends you $250,000/year of work.

Chapter III

Budgeting and Banking
Your Practice

The general mechanics and considerations involved in setting up a law office are described more thoroughly in other books, including Jay Foonberg's book *How To Start and Build a Law Practice*, now in its fifth edition and available through the American Bar Association. In this chapter, I discuss points that are particularly relevant to a real estate practice.

A. Budgeting Your Practice

People who would never go to a new city without a map will blithely start a new business without a budget. I cannot imagine how a lawyer can start a practice without some sort of budget. I invested two years in working on my business plan before I opened my own practice. The most important part of my business plan was the budget.

My budget was actually three budgets, all interrelated but each serving a different function. My first budget was my cost budget: what would it cost to open the doors? My cost budget included things such as my first month's rent and security deposit; the cost of telephone equipment; computers and routers; software for word processing, accounting, and billing; printers; letterhead and business cards; office supplies; tenant improvements for my office space; statute books; and the first year's insurance premiums. This first budget told me how much I would have to pay out to open the doors, a sum that I would have to raise through some combination of spending from my savings and borrowing from my lender.

My second budget was my expense budget, which I figured by starting with annual numbers and then allocating those expenses to the months in which I expected to pay them. Many monthly expenses are simply 1/12 of the annual expense. Rent and salaries are two good examples. Other expenses come at specific times of the year. I knew that bar dues and professional liability insurance premiums would be due in January and business taxes would be due in March, so I budgeted those expenses not in equal monthly installments but to fall in the months that they are actually due. I budgeted bonuses for my staff in June and December. I budgeted travel expenses for two annual conferences that I regularly attend in the months of those conferences. Whenever I could tie a particular expense to a particular month I budgeted that expense into that month. My finished budget had about 20 expense categories.

My third budget was my income budget. I budgeted myself to work a certain number of billable hours each month, not as 1/12 of my annual goal but with some adjustments based on what I knew I would be doing in specific months. I reduced my hours in February because it is a short month, in August because of an annual conference, and in December because of the holiday season. I increased my hours in March, July, and October. I did the same hours budget for my associate (I expected to hire one very soon after opening for business) and then converted the amounts to dollars.

I assumed that I would bill almost all time out in the month following: I would bill January's work in February, February's work in March, and so on. Because I had been in practice for 17 years before I opened my own office, I had available a long history—a long track record—of the interval between billing and payment and could rely on my clients continuing to pay promptly. Based on that track record, I figured that I would collect 50 percent of my invoices within a month after I sent them, 30 percent in the second month, and 15 percent in the third month. I figured that I would not collect the remaining 5 percent because the client had become unable or unwilling to pay, or because I would write down an account as a good-will gesture in response to a disappointing result.

Here is why your third budget must include not just how much you plan to bill out but when you expect to collect the fee. In my budget, if my office performed $50,000 of work in March that I billed in April, I could expect to collect for $25,000 of that work in April, $15,000 in May, and $5,000 in June. I did my initial income and expense budgets for a two-year period. I then combined the income and expense budgets to get my net cash flow. For the first few months, my overall budget was negative—more money would be going out than coming in, both because of the initial capital expenditures and because I would be paying expenses in cash before I would be collecting the associated accounts receivable. I added the total negative cash flow and my living expenses to my startup costs. The result was the total amount of cash that I had to have on hand in order to open for business and stay open until cash flow turned positive.

If you take the time and effort to prepare the three budgets for your practice, you will have a standard against which to measure whether your practice is meeting your expectations. If your net income is lower than you want and you don't have a budget, then you will not be able to tell whether it is because your billings are too low, or because your clients are paying more slowly than you expected, or because your expenses are too high. With a good set of budgets, you can identify and solve financial problems faster.

Here is what the first budget (the cost to open) might look like if you intend to open economically by subletting an office from another law firm, without staff or your own, using the copier and scanner of your landlord firm, and with the telephone connection and Internet service included in the rent:

Table III-1: Example of Cost Budget

Desk, chair, two guest chairs	$2,500
Computer, screen, two printers	4,000
Website design	1,500
First month's rent and deposit	1,500
Stationery	500
Office supplies	1,000
Filing cabinet or bookcase	500

Books, CDs, reference materials	1,000
Total	$12,500

If you are opening your practice by renting a room from an office suite company, you may not even need to buy the desk and chairs.

Your second budget (the expense budget) might be a larger version of something that looks like this table.

Table III-2: Example of Expense Budget

	January	February	March
Rent	$0 (because part of setup cost)	$750	$750
Phone and Internet	100	100	100
Bar dues	500	0	0
Insurance	3000	0	0
Supplies	150	150	150
Postage and FedEx	50	50	50
Advertising	500	0	0
Client development	200	200	200
Business licenses	0	100	0
Total	$4,500	$1,350	$$1,250

Your third budget (the income budget) when integrated with the first and second budgets might be a larger version of this table.

Table III-3: Example of Income Budget

	January	February	March
Billable time (in $)	$10,000	$15,000	$20,000
Bills mailed (in $)	0	10,000	15,000
Collections	0	5,000	10,500
Expenses (including first month's rent)	5,250	1,350	1,250

	January	February	March
Profit (loss)	(4,750)	3,650	9,250
YTD profit (loss)	(4,750)	(1,100)	8,150
Setup expenses	12,500	0	0
YTD cash flow	$(17,250)	$(13,600)	$(5,450)

Your actual budgets will be more detailed than these three tables and will cover a longer period of time. If you hire staff from the start, your expense budget will be larger. My setup and expense budgets included about 20 categories and covered a period of 24 months. My income budget also covered 24 months. Yours can be more or less detailed than mine as long as you understand them and can compare your performance to your budget.

One way to measure the efficiency of your practice is by its overhead. Overhead means all expenses except the salaries that you pay other attorneys and the profits you take home. If you are starting as a solo, you need less overhead than you think you do. If you work from a home office, with no staff, your overhead may be less than $10,000 a year. If you practice in a firm of 5 or 10 lawyers outside of the high-rent cities of New York and San Francisco, your overhead may be $100,000 to $125,000 per lawyer per year. Compare your overhead figure to the overhead of the national law firms, which is well above $200,000 per lawyer per year. Unlike an automobile factory or a software publishing house, a law firm does not have an efficiency of scale; beyond about 10 or 15 lawyers, the overhead cost per lawyer increases. Don't be surprised if when you budget your overhead expenses, you arrive at a figure for overhead per lawyer that's half or less of the overhead of the large firms in town.

B. Selecting Your Advisors

Assemble your team of advisors early on. You will already have a leasing agent, a real estate broker who advised you on leasing your space. You will also need an accountant to prepare your tax returns and tell you what returns you need to file. Choose an accountant the way you would want your clients to choose you as their lawyer. Is your accountant familiar with the needs of professional service firms? Is your accountant accessible by phone? Is the office convenient to yours? Does the accountant explain tax issues to you in a way that you understand?

Look for an accountant for your practice who advises clients in your target market. If you want real estate investors as clients, then look for an accountant who prepares tax returns for and advises real estate investors. If several of your clients use the same accountant and like the service they receive, use the same accountant for your firm.

If you aren't going to have an office manager or bookkeeper of your own, consider engaging a bookkeeping service to keep your books and records and assemble them for the accountant at tax time. Your accountant can recommend one.

If you have signed a multiyear lease and will be getting new carpeting, but you do not have an eye for color and design, hire a decorator to give you some help. You may be limited to building standard carpet, but you will have several colors from which to choose. A talented decorator may be able to warn you away from a color that looks attractive in a small swatch but that becomes overpowering in a hallway. Conversely, a pattern that looks disagreeably loud and ugly in a small swatch may become agreeably neutral in a hall or office. (I've been fooled twice that way by carpet samples. The third time around, I hired a professional decorator for advice on carpet and paint.)

Last but not least, you will need an insurance agent to locate and provide three kinds of coverage for your office. First is the equivalent of fire insurance for a renter: insurance against loss of or damage to your furnishings, files, and equipment. You can buy riders, or add-ons, to cover loss of income, cost to move if your space is burnt out, lease payments on substitute space, books and records, and the like.

Second is commercial general liability insurance, protecting you and your landlord against claims from people who are injured in your office. Standard office leases require tenants to carry commercial general liability insurance (called public liability insurance in older forms) and to name the landlord as an additional insured. Give your insurance agent a copy of the insurance provisions of your lease so that the policy will match the lease requirements.

Third is malpractice insurance (more formally called professional liability insurance), insurance to protect you against a client's claim that your work was negligent. Oregon is the only state that requires all lawyers in private practice to carry malpractice insurance. Every lawyer in private practice should carry malpractice insurance to protect their assets and pay for the cost of defense. The market for malpractice insurance is more specialized than the market for fire insurance and commercial general liability insurance. Your state bar association will have a list of carriers who are authorized to write policies in your state.

C. Selecting and Doing Business with Your Bank

1. Banking Is More than a Checking Account

As a business owner, you will have many important business relationships. One of the most important is with your bank. Your bank will provide more than just your business checking account. Its services to your practice can also include:

- Providing your client trust account, where you keep money that belongs to your clients;
- Maintaining separate client disbursement and payroll accounts, if you want to separate those functions from your general business account;
- Offering you a line of credit on which you can draw to pay your startup expenses and to cover bumps in your practice's cash flow;
- Issuing you a business credit card so that you can charge business expenses separately from personal expenses;
- Renting a safe deposit box;
- Receiving and sending domestic wire transfers;
- Receiving and sending foreign wire transfers;
- Processing clients' credit card payments for your fees;
- Financing your purchases of office equipment;
- Financing improvements to your office space;
- Serving as a trustee for your clients and their families; and
- Notarizing deeds and other documents for you and your clients.

The bank you choose should be one that's able to provide the services that you need for your practice, not just those that you need to start but those that you may need in the future. Don't build your main banking relationship with a bank that doesn't provide the services you need.

2. Three Factors to Weigh When You Choose Your Bank

Balance three factors to choose the right bank from among those that can provide the services you need. The first factor is the bank's location. Real estate investors say that the three most important factors in buying or leasing real estate are "location, location, and location." Location is only one factor when you're choosing your bank. If you will deposit paper checks at your bank, choose one that's convenient to your office. You or your assistant will be going to the bank several times a week; make the trip a short one. Because you'll go to the bank more often to deposit than to withdraw, if your bank offers electronic depositing, where you scan the checks and send the images to the bank, you can select a bank farther from your office because you won't be making many trips to the bank.

The second factor to consider is the size of the bank. Regional and national banks offer some services (e.g., sending and receiving overseas wire transfers through the SWIFT network) that many community banks don't. If you expect to transfer funds to or from clients in foreign countries, choose a bank that offers this service. On the other hand, at a large bank you will be a very small customer, and you will need to develop and nourish a good relationship with a bank officer.

If your clientele is mostly local, then interview the community banks in your area, especially any that have their main office in your city. You will be a more important customer at a small bank than you will be at a large bank. Obtain the names of the directors of your local banks—maybe you know one of the directors. Banks find their depositors and borrowers not just through general advertising but also through the efforts of their loan officers and relationship managers. Small banks also obtain business through their directors in a way that larger banks don't. You will have some cachet if you're introduced to a loan officer by one of the bank directors.

If you will hold more funds for a single client in your lawyer trust account than the FDIC insurance limit (currently $250,000), then you should also evaluate the bank's financial strength when you are depositing those funds. Under current law, lawyer trust accounts generally qualify for pass-through deposit insurance coverage with each client's share calculated separately, as long as the bank's records indicate that the account is a trust or fiduciary account, and as long as you keep regular business records that indicate the portions of the account funds that belong to each of your clients. Pass-through coverage means that if the bank fails, the FDIC will measure each client's insurance coverage independently based on the client's share of the account. For example, if your trust account has $100,000 from each of five clients, for a total trust balance of $500,000, then the trust account will be treated for deposit insurance purposes as if it were five separate accounts of $100,000 for each of the five clients.

The third factor to consider is the bank's willingness to provide financing to your clients. Real estate investors like to borrow money. I often have clients ask if I can introduce them to lenders, and both the clients and the lenders appreciate the introductions. Bankers want referrals as much as lawyers do. This factor is in some tension with the second factor; you will be a more important customer at a smaller bank, but a smaller bank may not provide the range of real estate loans that your clients want. Deposit your business funds with a bank that wants to do business with your real estate clients.

Chapter IV

Selecting a Location

This chapter discusses how to select a community (city, suburb, or town) in which to set up your practice, and then how to select a location (neighborhood) within the town, and then how to select the type of office (storefront, high-rise, shared office, home office). A complete discussion of how to choose your office space and negotiate your lease would fill a book. This chapter and Chapter V are not a complete discussion of how to lease an office, but they do offer a few helpful tips for choosing and leasing an office for your real estate practice.

A. Choose a Community and a Location

The first question you must decide is in what town, or what part of town, you would like to have your office. Your office should be reasonably convenient to where you live, but it also needs to be convenient to the clients who will come to your office. Unless you like driving, don't rent an office so far away from home that you will come to detest the time and energy you spend to commute. Time in the car is not very productive. I've never lived more than 20 minutes from my office.

In any field of law, you will have an advantage in setting up your practice in your home town, or where you've lived and made connections, or where you attended school, because you have a head start on meeting people and building your network, compared to lawyers who move to the area without connections or introductions. Because real estate practice is so intensely local, it's one of the rare fields of law in which you get a substantive benefit, and not just a marketing benefit, from setting up shop in your home town. If you know the progress of urban development, the major landowners, the zoning structure, and the history and market for certain classes of local real estate because you've observed these things for five or ten or twenty years before you were admitted to the bar, you will begin your practice with far more product knowledge than someone of equal legal experience who has just moved to your town. In other fields of law, the hometown advantage will speed your marketing and networking efforts, but it doesn't contribute to your knowledge of the industry. So if you haven't settled on a city in which to practice, start by evaluating your hometown as a place to live and work.

Because real estate is so intensely local, the longer you practice in a city, the more you will come to know about the real estate industry there, and the less mobile you will become later in your career. A tax lawyer with 20 years of experience in San Francisco who moves to San Antonio will still have 20 years of experience dealing with and interpreting the federal tax laws and can use that experience for the benefit of clients in San Antonio, even if he or she must rebuild a marketing network and client base. But a real estate lawyer with 20 years of experience in Portland, Oregon, who moves to Portland, Maine, will not only have to learn a new set of state laws but will also restart without knowing anything about the local market. So pick your town or city carefully when you start out.

Within your city, you may have a wide choice of neighborhoods in which to open your office. A town of 5,000 or 10,000 people will have only one center: one core office area, usually near city hall, the courthouse, and (if it's the county seat) the county recorder. A city of 100,000 people will have not only a downtown with buildings of five to ten floors but also several suburban office clusters near major intersections. And a metropolitan area of 1,000,000 or more people will have a downtown core, several suburbs or bedroom communities, and some cities that are business centers in their own right. In a large metropolitan area, you will have a lot of choices for your office, not just among different spaces to lease but also among different communities.

When I was choosing a location for my office in 2006, I wanted a location that my clients could find and drive to easily. My largest clients were not concentrated in any particular part of town; some were downtown, some were in other areas of the city, and some were in the suburbs. On grounds of convenience, I narrowed my choices to two. One choice was to be in any of several office towers in downtown Portland that were close to the courthouse and the title insurance companies and that had parking within the building. The other choice was a suburban office park, recently constructed, that was a three-minute walk from a light rail station that in turn was 10 minutes from downtown. The office park had ample free parking and was at the junction of two freeways; I could easily describe to clients how to come to my office whether they would arrive by car or by train. I looked at three downtown buildings that met my requirements and ultimately chose one that was a three-minute walk or less to the courthouse, the title companies, my bank, bus, and light rail. I could get to the services I needed, and my clients and employees could get to my office. My choice had the additional benefit that one of my longtime clients owned the building and was pleased that I would be increasing his gross revenues. (See Section XVII.C, "How and When to Do Business with Your Clients.")

The economy goes up and down, but in some areas it has been going generally up, and in other areas it has been going generally down. Look for an area where the population has been increasing, or at least staying stable. More growth means more demand for your services.

B. Choose a Type of Building That Fits with the Practice You Want

When you have selected a part of town for your office, next consider what kind of building you want to be in. The type of building you choose will depend on many things, two of which are your budget and tastes. In choosing a building, you should also consider the type of client and business that you want to attract. If you plan to do a lot of residential real estate closings, you will want an office that is visible from the street, probably a building where you can have your name on the outside, where passing drivers can see your sign and your building. If your goal is to do a lot of repeat business with the same clients, then being visible from the street is less important.

Once your clients have come to your office, they will know where it is and be able to find it again without relying on a sign. And as our taste for electronic communication increases, clients come to the office less and less often.

For a business practice, pick a location where it's easy for your clients to come see you, and from which you can easily go see your clients. Can you describe how to get to your office? Is it accessible by public transit? Is ample parking available? Think of how you choose to buy groceries. Do you ever go to a particular store not because the quality is better or the prices lower, but simply because it's easier to get in and out? Some of your clients think the same when they choose a lawyer.

If you rent space where there is a charge for parking, as in a downtown office tower with a pay parking lot or structure, then I suggest that you validate clients' parking tickets. People can be reluctant to come downtown and pay $5 or $10 for parking just to see their lawyer (who is expensive enough already), but be more willing to consult you if the parking is free. Your goal as a lawyer is to encourage your clients to see you and call you more often, rather than less. Don't be put off by paying the cost of parking. Whenever you pay $10 to buy a client two hours of parking, the client is paying you much more than that for your time and expertise.

Depending on your practice, your location may need to be convenient to more than just you and your clients. Is it close to a bank that will handle your business and trust accounts? Is it close to title insurance and escrow companies that will handle your clients' transactions? Is it close to the county clerk's office? If you expect to ship documents out of town often, then you will want to be close to a FedEx pickup station or on a route for FedEx or UPS.

I've divided the range of possible offices into five basic types: the storefront office, the tower office, the office sublet from another lawyer or shared with other lawyers, the room in a general office suite, and the home office.

1. The Street-Level (Storefront) Office

I'm using the term "storefront office" to mean an office that clients enter directly from the street, without passing through a building lobby or riding an elevator. Being at street level may be right for your practice. If you have a street-level building on a busy street, thousands of people a day will pass by your sign. Even if they do not remember your name from your sign, they will come to know that a lawyer is in that building. From time to time, they will have legal needs, and it will occur to some of them to go visit the lawyer's office they have driven past. Having a visible storefront office is more useful to a consumer practice—a practice that relies mainly on clients who come for a single transaction—than to a business practice where most of the work comes from repeat clients who have already engaged you on other matters and who know how to find you. Some storefront offices have signs that identify the lawyer or the firm, and others are marked with signs that display the generic term "LAW OFFICE."

The storefront itself can be one of your advertisements. The San Francisco law office of the late Melvin Belli, the "King of Torts," even became a tourist attraction. Passers-by could look through the plate glass window and see him and his associates at work.

A storefront office will convey the message that you are approachable and easy to reach. Some prospective clients will see the sign and walk in without an appointment just as they would enter a retail store, so if you open a storefront office, you will need a receptionist to greet, intercept, and screen unscheduled visitors. Also, because your workspaces will be in view of the public, you and your staff will need to be vigilant to keep confidential documents away from the street windows.

In choosing a storefront office that is part of a strip center with a shared parking lot, look at the signage carefully. Will you be able to have a sign for your office on a shared monument or pylon sign by the street that drivers can see from a distance, well before they turn into the driveway to your parking area? Is it obvious to drivers who see your sign which of several commercial driveways they should turn into? Your clients will become irritated and annoyed if they can see your office sign only after they've passed the entrance to your parking lot.

If your center does not have a shared pylon or monument sign, or if you are renting too small of an office to get a space on the sign, you should nevertheless consider what signage the center does have. Even if you can't have your office name on the pylon sign, if there is a pylon sign with the name of the center (let's say it's the Acme Center), you can at least tell your clients to look for the pylon sign that says "Acme Center" and where the driveway is in relation to that sign.

2. The Tower Office

I'm using the term "tower office" to include offices in a wide range of buildings, but with the common element that your office is above the ground floor and is reached through a common building lobby that serves all of the building's office tenants. Some "tower offices" are on the second floor of a two-floor building. Others are 20, 40, 60, or 80 floors above the street. Some tower offices are in old buildings that range from the well-maintained grandes dames of your city down to the frankly shabby. Others are in modern class A skyscrapers of glass and steel.

The higher you are and the newer the building, the more expensive your rent will be, and the higher your clients will expect your fees to be. (Having your clients expect you to charge high fees is not always good.) Some clients will connect the quality of your services to the quality of your office space. Others will jump to the conclusion, based on your location alone, that they can't afford your services.

One benefit of a tower office is the added security that comes with your office being above street level and from the building elevators and possibly the lobby also being locked to the public at night.

3. The Sublet or Shared Law Office

An alternative to leasing and furnishing your own office is to rent space from a law firm or to share space with other solo practitioners. Many law firms have unused rooms that they are willing to rent out. The advantage of renting a room from an established firm is that you will usually get receptionist service, the use of the coffee machine, telephone cabling, and access to a conference room and copier. You may also get occasional overflow work from the firm or referrals for client conflicts. A disadvantage is that you are in an office space with the name of another law firm on the door, and you must be careful to explain to your clients that although you rent space from the firm, you are not part of the firm. (The firm will also want to make sure its clients know that you are not a member of the firm.) If you rent space from a firm, get your own telephone number so that your calls will be answered with your business name and not with an anonymous "Law Offices." So that you can fulfill your duty of confidentiality to your clients, confirm that you will have a secure area in which to store your client files, not accessible to the other lawyers who work in the same suite, or invest in some locking file cabinets of your own that can be placed in the shared file room.

One advantage of the sublet or shared law office is that your startup costs can be very small. The infrastructure (walls, doors, cabling, and break room) will already be in place. You don't have to lease or buy your own copier. You may be able to use the firm's law library instead of buying your own books. Another advantage is that the lawyers in the office who don't work in real estate may refer real estate clients to you simply because you're convenient to them.

A disadvantage is that if the firm adds lawyers you will be pushed out to make room for them. If you do rent an office from a firm, either ask for a fixed-term lease (maybe one year to start) or for 60 or 90 days' advance notice if the firm terminates your lease to make room for a new employee. Thirty days is not enough time to move your practice if you're in the middle of a large project.

If you rent space from an established firm or group of solo practitioners and your office will not be large enough for meeting with clients, confirm how often the conference room is booked, and how much access you'll have to it. You can't have an eight-person meeting in your office if the one room that will accommodate eight people is always in use.

4. The Commercial Shared Office Suite

Instead of renting an office from a law firm, you can rent an office from an office suite company, one that operates office suites with private offices available for rent by the hour, day, week, or month. Regus USA (http://www.regus.com) is one of several companies that operates office space, meeting rooms, "virtual offices" (see section 6 below), and other workspaces in major cities. Servcorp (http://www.servcorp.com) is another. You can rent a room that will be all your own, and you can buy almost any mix of office services that you want. The operator provides a receptionist, an Internet connection, meeting rooms, and telecommunications connections. It's easy to lease space and easy to end your lease.

Against the convenience of easy entry and exit are some disadvantages. Because you share the space with long-term and occasional tenants, the reception area will remain unbranded. That's good, in that you won't appear to be a subtenant in someone else's office, but not so good, in that the space won't be marked as being yours either. You also won't have space for a physical law library, though having a physical law library is becoming less important as more information moves online.

As with the sublet or shared office, examine how easily you can book a conference room. I suggest visiting the shared office suite several times before you sign a lease, at different times of the day and on different days of the week, just to note whether its conference rooms are full or available.

5. The Home Office

Another choice, if you don't expect clients to come see you in person, is to set your office up in your home. A home office can work if you don't need any staff.

I have several recommendations for you if you should decide to open your office at home. First, don't scrimp on technology. We live in a wired world, and your clients need to be able to get in touch with you even if they aren't going to come visit you in person. Get a separate telephone number for your home office, for your business use only, and tell your family that they cannot make personal calls from your office telephone. Many people have Caller ID on their telephones and return calls to the number that shows on the screen. When your family places personal calls on your office phone, the personal return calls will start to come to your office phone.

Second, place your home office in an entire room that you can close, and not a corner of a room that you share with your family. Even though you will be working in your home, when you are inside the room, you should consider yourself to be just as much in the office at work as if your office was located somewhere else. If you share the room with your family (e.g., if it's the room where you keep toys and games, or a room that must be passed through to go between the kitchen and the laundry room), then your work will be interrupted, and you won't be able to ensure that your phone calls with clients are private and confidential.

The people you live with need to understand that your office is your private space and must agree not to knock on or open the door of your office while you are meeting with a client unless an emergency has occurred. Be very clear about what is an emergency. The house catching fire is an emergency; your child being hurt and needing to be taken to the hospital is an emergency; someone wanting to know if you've seen the car keys is not an emergency. Otherwise, the stream of interruptions will make it very difficult for you to get your work done.

If you don't live alone, then the door to your home office should have a lock. If you keep your files in a different room, either that area should have a lock or the file cabinet should have a lock. The lock does not need to be taken from a bank vault; its purposes are to protect client confidences from the casual curiosity of others and to reinforce the message to your family that when you are in your office working, you are not home; you are at work just as if you had an office in an office building.

You will have to set some boundaries with your clients also. Just as your family must understand that when you are in your home office, you are actually at work, so too must your clients understand that when you are home but not in your home office, you are not at work. Clients who know that you work from your home may figure that if you don't answer your work phone (the separate line that rings in your office), they can call you at your home number. From the client's point of view, your two telephone numbers are simply different lines that ring in the same house. And since you work from home, you should in the client's mind be available to take work calls whenever you're home, because isn't your office just down the hall from where you're answering the telephone?

One way to reduce the problem of the unreasonable client is to record a message on your office phone that is the same message that you would record if you worked in an office building. Your voice mail message can direct clients who call after hours to send you an e-mail or (if you're willing) to call your cell phone. If your local telephone company offers a voice mail service that you can access from phones other than your office phone, and if you install only one telephone line to your office, then I recommend that you subscribe to that service instead of buying an answering machine for your office line. First, the sound quality of the systems used by telephone companies is usually very good, better than an answering machine. Second, the telephone company's voice mail will answer a call and take a message when you are on the telephone. An answering machine in your house won't answer a telephone call while you're using the line, and the caller will get only a busy signal. Your telephone technology should assure you that during business hours, no call will go unanswered (even if the call goes directly to voice mail) and no caller will get a busy signal.

Before you set your office up in your home, confirm that the local zoning code will allow you to conduct a home occupation there. If your neighborhood has recorded covenants, conditions, and restrictions, verify that the covenants don't prohibit you from practicing law from your house. You won't usually have a zoning issue with working from home if no employees work at your home and no clients come to see you at your home, but it can become a problem with the zoning authorities or with your neighborhood association if you hire staff who come to your home to work, or if clients regularly come to see you at home. You don't want to be highlighted in the local newspaper as the real estate lawyer who didn't read the zoning code.

6. The Virtual Office?

If you choose to have a home office, one surprisingly affordable enhancement is to add a virtual office, meaning a location that provides you with a street address, telephone service, and a receptionist, but where you don't have the use of the actual space. The staff of the virtual office will handle your mail and answer your calls, providing you with the image of a physical presence without your actually being there. You can rent meeting rooms as you need them. The combination of a home office and virtual office will allow you to use a business address and telephone on your letterhead and court filings instead of your home address and telephone, and to make appointments to meet with your clients in a business location, keeping your files and computers in your home office. If you do not want the walk-in traffic that a storefront office would generate, and if you're opening your practice on a tight budget, you can come close to the impression of having your own physical office by keeping your physical office at home and using the virtual office for your address and telephone.

Chapter V

Leasing and Furnishing Your Office

A. Choose Your Lease Length Wisely

How long should your first lease be? The answer depends on your plans for the space. If you are starting out in a home office, then you don't need a lease at all. But if you are beginning your practice in a building that you don't own, then you should insist on some kind of written rental agreement no matter how cordial your relations are with the owner. A written agreement will protect you and your landlord from misunderstandings later on, and if your state has adopted the common-law statute of frauds, then if your rental agreement is for a period longer than one year, it will need to be in writing to be enforceable.

If you view your first office as a stopgap, a temporary location while you decide the longer-term goal for your practice, then rent space from an office-sharing firm or another law firm. The office-sharing firm will explain at the start what notice (usually one month, sometimes even less) you have to give in order to terminate your lease. The office-sharing firm is unlikely to terminate your lease unless you are a truly troublesome tenant, but you should make sure you will be given at least a month's notice if the landlord wants to terminate your lease or raise your rent.

If you are leasing an office from a law firm, your lease will probably be month to month. Ask for 60 days' notice, or longer, if the law firm wants to terminate your lease to make room for a new employee. Your law firm landlord will understand the time required to move a law practice.

You can lease a storefront or tower office month to month, but you will be at the risk of a more valued tenant coming along and outbidding you for the space. If you expect your first location to be more than temporary, then I suggest starting with at least a three-year lease. If you commit to a three-year lease, then the landlord will offer at least some modest tenant improvements beyond paint and carpeting. You can have a space that looks fresh, even in an old building, and you won't have to worry that a higher bidder will come along and induce your landlord to switch tenants before the lease term expires.

If you want your office to be a long-term location, then instead of leasing month to month you should lease the space for a fixed period so that you will not unexpectedly have to move if the landlord finds a higher-paying tenant. Another reason to sign a lease for several years is that you will get full value out of the painting, carpeting, decorating, and equipment installation. When I opened my firm, I signed a five-year lease. That gave me the security to make the space look how I wanted it to look. It also meant that I could install equipment and furniture knowing that I would get five years' use of it in that space without having to move it.

If you are nervous about taking on a long-term commitment to a landlord because of the chance that you might become disabled during the term of the lease and leave your family with an expensive commitment to your landlord, then you can buy disability insurance to cover that risk, or ask the landlord to include a provision in the lease that if you become unable to practice law, you can cancel the lease on payment of a modest termination fee.

B. Understand the Flavors of Rent: Gross, Full-Service, Net, Triple-Net

If you regularly handle office and retail leases, then you can pass over this section. If you haven't represented landlords and tenants in negotiating leases, then reading and negotiating your office lease will give you some practical experience in the leasing world while you are looking out for your own interests.

Apartment rents are simple. If the rent is $900/month, then every month you pay the landlord $900. You would pay utility providers separately for gas, electricity, and telephone, but the stated rent is all that you pay your landlord each month.

Unless you rent a room from a law firm or an office suite company, understanding your rent is not so simple. The actual rent you pay may be what's stated in your lease, or it may be what's stated in your lease plus a share of the operating costs for the building.

What your rent is, and how it will change over the term of your lease, depends on how your rent is figured. The simplest form of rent is gross rent. It's the same as apartment rent: In exchange for paying $X per month, you have the use of a certain space. The landlord provides heat, light, and other utilities except communications. As long as you continue to pay $X/month, you will be able to occupy the space for the term of the lease.

In the office world, full-service leases are common. Rent that is quoted as full-service rent is the same as gross rent, but only for the first year. After that, the landlord passes along to you (charges you for) a share of the increase in the landlord's cost to operate the building compared to the first year. For example, if you lease a space for $1000/month, full service, which is 10 percent of the leasable area in the building, and if the landlord's property taxes and operating costs for the first year are $40,000, then in the second year in addition to the $1000/month (called the "base rent"), you will pay 10 percent of the amount by which the landlord's operating costs surpass $40,000. If the landlord's operating costs are $43,000 then you will pay an additional $25/month, or $300/year, as your share of that increase. The "full service" name conveys the idea that the rent covers the use of the space and all utility services, which is true, but only for the first year.

It used to be common to write leases with net rent, called "net leases," in which in addition to the base rent, the tenant pays a proportionate share of the property taxes. In our example, if the property taxes on the building are $15,000/year and you agree to pay $1000/month net, then in addition to the $1000/month ($12,000/year), you would pay $1500/year as your 10 percent share of the property taxes.

More common now than the net lease is the "triple-net lease," often abbreviated to "NNN lease" or a lease with "NNN rent." In a triple-net lease, you reimburse the landlord for your share of the taxes, insurance, and operating expenses in addition to your base rent. So in our example where the taxes and operating costs are $40,000/year, if you lease the space for $1,000/month triple-net, in addition to the base rent, you would pay the landlord 10 percent of the $40,000 each year, usually spread over 12 monthly installments.

Spaces in larger buildings are sometime leased on a full-service basis and sometimes on a triple-net basis. If you're comparing rents in different buildings, make sure that the landlords are quoting rent the same way (either both full-service or both triple-net), or adjust your comparison to take account of the difference. Again, the rent on a full-service lease includes the property taxes, utilities, and building operating costs for the first year, but the rent on a triple-net lease doesn't—you pay those costs in addition to the stated rent. Consider two identical buildings for which the taxes, insurance, and operating costs are both $6/square foot/year. If you're offered space in one building for $15/square foot triple-net and space in the other building at $19/square foot full-service, the full-service building is actually cheaper than the triple-net building even though the quoted rent is $4/square foot more. The higher rent of $19 is actually cheaper than the $15 rent because if you rent space in the triple-net building, you will pay not only the $15 rent charge but an additional $6/square foot for operating costs, bringing your total rent to $21/square foot per year.

C. Know What the Landlord Provides

In an apartment lease, the tenant can assume that the landlord will provide basic services—heat, electricity, and hot and cold running water—as required by law. This is not the case in an office lease. If it isn't in the contract, your landlord doesn't have to do it. Your lease should state what services the landlord will provide.

1. Heat and Light/After-Hours Services
The lease should require the landlord to provide heat and electricity (sometimes called "heat and light" in older lease forms). Because most offices

aren't occupied around the clock, it's usual for the landlord to promise to provide heating (and, if the building has air conditioning, cooling) during defined business hours and to provide electricity and electric connections sufficient for ordinary business use 24 hours a day, seven days a week. If your space does not have separately metered electricity and gas service, or if it doesn't have thermostats that allow you to control the heating and cooling, then ask for a provision that requires the landlord to provide heating (and cooling, if available) to you after hours and on weekends for a specified charge per hour.

2. Signage

Whether you have an artist or craftsperson make a hanging sign with your name and a quill pen, or you put up a plain sign that reads "LAW OFFICES," you will almost certainly want some signs to identify your office. In a storefront office, your sign might be a blade (flat hanging sign) at the door, your name painted on the door or window, or a simple brass plate. Make sure the lease allows you to do that.

In a tower office, the landlord will have building standard signage for the main lobby, the individual floor elevator lobbies, and the individual tenant doors. The lease should include a provision requiring the landlord to provide you with building standard signage in these locations.

If you are renting a storefront in a building with a parking lot and monument sign, ask for signage on the monument sign.

3. Parking

How much your lease needs to say about parking depends on your office location. If you rent a room from a law firm or shared office suite, your lease may say nothing about parking because your landlord doesn't own the building and doesn't control the parking at the building. If you open your office in an urban storefront or in an office tower with no parking, your lease will say nothing about parking because the landlord doesn't have any parking to offer you.

If you open your office in a suburban building with a large common parking lot, all your lease needs to say about parking is that you and your clients and employees may park in the parking lot in common with the other tenants and their customers, without any separate charge. To keep the spaces next to the building available for customers, the landlord may require your employees to park in designated spaces, or to park away from the building. Landlords more commonly require tenants' employees to park away from the building in shopping centers than in buildings that are entirely offices. If your office is in a downtown office tower that has paid parking only, ask in your lease for the right to rent a monthly parking space in the tower. You should expect to be able to rent one monthly space for every 1,000 square feet or so of your office.

Also look for a commitment that the landlord or the landlord's parking operator will have a system that will allow you to validate and pay for your clients' parking tickets.

4. Janitorial

If you rent an office from a law firm or an office suite company, then janitorial service will be provided, at least at the level of removing trash and vacuuming the floors. Long-form office leases usually contain specific statements of the janitorial services that the landlord will provide. Here is an example of a janitorial clause that favors the tenant:

> Landlord shall supply all janitorial and maintenance service required to maintain the Premises in a first class condition, including (without limitation) daily janitorial service, periodic carpet shampooing and tile cleaning, interior and supplemental exterior window cleaning, trash removal and light bulb, tube and ballast replacements.

A similar clause that favors the landlord will provide specific performance standards instead of requiring the landlord to provide "all janitorial and maintenance service." Here is one janitorial clause:

> Landlord will provide janitorial service consisting of trash removal five days a week, regular vacuuming of carpets and floors, replacement of light bulbs, and exterior window cleaning.

If you rent a storefront, then you may have to engage your own janitorial company to clean and vacuum. Your lease will include a clause that assigns responsibility for cleaning the outside windows, and if that responsibility is yours, then delegate that task to your janitorial service also. Establish a regular time for your janitorial service so that its work won't conflict with your client meetings.

5. Security

An important factor to consider when choosing your office space is security, both to protect your office equipment and data from theft and to protect the confidences and secrets of your clients. An office in an office tower is likely to be more secure than a storefront office because the tower office has two or three layers of locking: one at the main entrance, another at your office door, and possibly one in between if the elevators are controlled by access cards after hours. The storefront office may have only one layer of locking (the street door) and can be entered by breaking a window.

Larger office towers will have some level of 24-hour security such as round-the-clock guard service. The guards will divide their time between a guard station in the lobby and patrols of the building corridors. The guards will be backed up by video monitoring. Smaller buildings won't have employees on site around the clock and may have less sophisticated monitoring systems. Because security and monitoring are operating costs that landlords recover in the rent they charge, your rent will be higher at a building with better security. You get what you pay for.

A slightly different part of building security is how comfortable you and your staff will feel when you are working before or after hours or on weekends. An empty building can be a spooky place on a Saturday morning in January. You and your coworkers will feel safer working in a building that has 24-hour staffing.

6. Communications Connections

A newer building will brag about its communications connections and how easily you can get telephone and Internet access to each floor. An older building may be more discreet. In view of how important it will be for you to have high-speed Internet access, not just for your e-mail but also for access to online data, legal research services, court filings, and zoning maps and codes, confirm that high-speed Internet service is available to your office space before you sign the lease. The day after you sign your lease is not a good time to learn that it's going to cost you an extra $2,000 to run new communications cable from the nearest demarcation point (the point where the public telephone network ends and connects to private wiring) to your office space itself.

D. Understanding Your Office Lease

When you have found the right office, you are ready to negotiate the lease. If you expect your office to be a short-term location, then a month-to-month lease may be fine. I suggest you ask the landlord to give you 60 or 90 days' notice of termination, instead of 30 days, because it takes time and effort to change offices and 30 days is a very short time in which to find a new location, negotiate and sign a lease, arrange for movers, and relocate your files, furniture, and telephone connections.

Be clear in the lease about which services are included in the rent that you are paying. In smaller buildings, electricity is sometimes separately metered to the individual tenant spaces, meaning that your rent doesn't pay for your entire cost to be in the building.

One advantage of renting space in a building with many small tenants is that if you need more space, the landlord can often find you a larger space in the same building by moving one of your neighbors to another space in the building.

The flip side of being in a building where the landlord can move one tenant to make room for another is that the landlord may want to move your office to make room for one of your neighbors to expand into your suite. A relocation clause in your lease allows the landlord to move you to a comparable space in the building, possibly with a downward adjustment in rent if the space is less desirable, and with the landlord paying your relocation costs. Whether the space is less desirable will be for you and the landlord to discuss. You may have picked your suite to be on one side of the building so that you will have a view of the mountains, and discover a year or two later that the landlord wants to move your office to the opposite side of the building, facing the freeway. As a small tenant in a large building, you probably won't be able to negotiate the relocation clause to be entirely out of the lease, but you may be able to negotiate some limits, for example, agreeing that the replacement space will be on a floor no lower than your initial floor and will be no smaller than your initial space. If you do agree to a relocation clause, make sure that the landlord promises to build out the replacement space to the same quality and level as your initial space.

If you are fortunate, you will find an office space that is ready to move into. More often the space will require painting and carpeting, and possibly some other work, to make it suit your needs. If you sign a long-term lease, then the landlord will pay part of the cost to remodel the space for your office, but only if you negotiate that contribution in the lease itself. It's usually called a tenant improvement allowance. Do not sign the lease and then hope that the landlord will give you money to improve the office. As there is no free lunch, the more work you want the landlord to pay for, the higher the rent will be.

If you plan to work on weekends, then you will sometimes want your office to be heated or cooled on weekends. If your electricity and natural gas are separately metered, then you will have control of the heating and cooling of your office. If you are in a larger building, you may not be able to turn the heating and cooling on when you wish, but will be limited to the landlord's standard hours of operation. Landlords will provide heating and cooling on the weekends, but for a charge. If your office won't have its own thermostat and temperature control, be sure that your lease states whether the landlord will heat and cool your office on the weekends if you ask and, if so, what the extra charge to you will be.

E. Design and Furnish Your Office Space Carefully

If you are renting space from an office services company, then your landlord will provide most of your office furnishings. If you are renting a suite, then you will have to consider how to design and furnish your space.

Your office space has to fulfill several needs. It should include a comfortable place for you to work (usually your desk in your private office), workspaces for your staff, a reception area for clients, a conference area in which you can meet with clients, an area to store files, an area with a water line for making coffee and tea, a work area for copying and assembling documents, and storage for files and office supplies. If you are starting your own office, parts of your suite may serve several purposes. One room may accommodate file storage, office supplies, copying, and the coffeemaker. Your private office may double as your conference room. Whether you need to start out with a separate conference room will depend on your practice, including whether you expect to handle real estate closings, in which case you will often have more people at a closing than can comfortably sit around your desk. In my state, most real estate sales are closed at the offices of title and escrow companies. In 25 years of practice, I've handled only one real estate closing myself. Local customs differ widely. If in your area property sales are handled at lawyers' offices and you expect to close real estate transactions where the parties all gather around the same table, then you will need either a "closing room" in your office suite, or to share space with, or rent space from, a firm that has a common conference room that you can use for signings and closings. Whichever the case, you should have access to a room that is suitable for at least six people to sit comfortably and that doesn't contain client files and confidential documents. You don't want Client A to spot a file or paper that indicates what property Client B is purchasing.

If you will not handle closings in your office, then your office needs are simpler. You will still need a place to meet with clients, which can be your office or a shared conference room. If you do not belong to the school of clean desks, then I recommend having a conference or other meeting place available so that your clients will not see papers of your other clients on your desk. Some office buildings offer a common conference room for the use of all tenants, and if you rent space in a building with this amenity, you can get by with only a small conference room in your suite, relying on the building's conference room for larger meetings.

If the landlord will be installing new walls or relocating existing walls to build out your space, insist that the landlord's contractor install insulation in all of the walls. The reason for the insulation is not to conserve energy, but to dampen sound. Office equipment is quieter than it was 30 years ago, but office workers aren't. You need to be concerned about sound if your officemate is addicted to the speakerphone or if your suite is next to a louder business. Some sound insulation will make your room more pleasant, and it will also assist in protecting your client confidences. If you can hear your neighbor talk, then your neighbor can hear you talk.

If you're adding walls to your suite, install extra communications cable and connections. It's cheap to install extra wiring and connections before the drywall goes up. We installed two phone ports and two data ports in each office when we designed our space, in case communications needs increase in the future.

For your file storage, I suggest buying open steel file shelves rather than cabinets with pull-out drawers. The file shelves can be taller and require less space because you don't have to allow room for any drawers to pull out. Good file shelves will have protective doors on tracks that slide up to be stored above each shelf of files when not in use and that you can pull out at night to protect your files from water damage if the building sprinklers go off.

As for your overall office décor, even if your suite is clean and functional rather than a showplace, have one unusual item that reinforces your marketing. In my first office, I selected a deep green for the walls to complement one of the building standard carpet colors. The overall effect was subdued, except for one item: In the reception area I installed a floor-to-ceiling mural that was a real estate company's map of Portland from the 1890s, advertising a new subdivision. The Oregon Historical Society provided the map, and a local printing company printed it on vinyl wallpaper. Many of my clients and other visitors, waiting for their appointment, would turn around, study the map, and look for their neighborhood. It was a simple and effective conversation piece and cost me less than $1,000 to manufacture and hang. It also reemphasized the message that mine was a real estate practice.

F. Striving for Stability

Even if you do not take on a long-term commitment and sign a one- or two-year lease for your first office, it's a good idea to ask if the landlord will consider a longer lease when your initial lease expires. It's time-consuming to look for new space and organize a move, and it's expensive to pay for a move. You will pay for the moving company, of course, but you will also pay for new stationery, new furniture (if the old furniture doesn't fit your new space), overtime fees to the landlord's staff to open the building for your move-out and move-in, and the other odd expenses that crop up. You will also spend your time managing the move, which is time in which you cannot do paying work for your clients, and your clients won't be able to reach you. After you've completed your move, you will have to reeducate your clients about your new location. Unless your building becomes unsuitable for your business, you will save a lot of out-of-pocket costs and opportunity costs by choosing an office space and an office building that can accommodate you for many years.

You won't build steady business from repeat clients if they don't know where and how to find you. If you haven't established your reputation in the community yet, you will build it much faster if you stay in one location for several years than if you move from one month-to-month lease to another or shift your location by 10 or 20 miles. If you are in a small town, your clients will understand why you are moving from one space in that town to another space in the same town. If you are moving because you've hired more staff or an associate and you've outgrown your office, you can use your move as a marketing opportunity—send "We're growing!" postcards to your clients to announce the move and invite them to an office warming celebration when you're established in your new space.

Your clients are less likely to understand why you're moving if you move from one town to another, and they're much less likely to follow you. Some of your clients may not have chosen you just because your office is convenient to their office, but if you move 20 miles farther away they may come across another lawyer who seems equally expert, located five minutes from their offices. Clients who didn't choose you because your office is convenient may slowly stop sending you work if your new office is inconvenient.

In his 1947 book *Advice to a Young Solicitor*, H. O. Lock wrote, accurately if not diplomatically, "Customers, and for that matter presumably clients, in their habits as affecting goodwill have been aptly likened to dogs, cats, rabbits and rats. Dogs attach themselves to persons; cats to places;

rabbits feed near home, while rats are indiscriminate." If you move your office often and far, the dogs will follow you, but the cats and rabbits will take their business to another lawyer. Stay in one place so that the cats and rabbits stay with you.

Chapter VI

Supplying Your Office

A. Letterhead, Business Cards, and Other Stationery

Lawyers have traditionally used engraved stationery and business cards. Engraved cards and stationery convey a message of stability. My first business cards, in 1989, were traditional in form: black text engraved on white cardstock, with no logotypes or other artwork. My cards stated my name, address, telephone and facsimile numbers, and firm name. Websites and e-mail had not yet arrived on the scene, and no other information was necessary except the modest phrase "Attorney at law."

What is traditional is no longer common. Lawyers and law firms have taken to color and logotypes, and rare is the letterhead without a design, an embossment, or a splash of color. Lawyers have become more debonair in their stationery as well as their advertising.

Whatever your taste in stationery may be, make your letterhead and business cards consistent with the clients that you want to serve, and with one another. Established suppliers of stationery to attorneys such as Stuart F. Cooper (http://www.sfcooper.com), H.A. Friend & Company (http://www.friendsstationery.com), and Tuttle Printing & Engraving (http://www.tuttleprinting.com) will assist you with laying out and designing your stationery and business cards, either free or at very low cost, in exchange for your orders. Suppliers of legal stationery will send you sample books that show different combinations of paper, printing method, design, and ink for you to consider.

If you do not have an eye for design, take advantage of the skills and experience of someone who does, either through your printer or by hiring a designer who understands layout and typography. A small design fee is inexpensive for a design that you will be using for 20 years or more.

Choose white or very light off-white paper for your letterhead, with matching envelopes. Darker paper colors are attractive, but they don't photocopy or scan well. A background color that is unobtrusive in the original may turn into a London pea-soup fog when copied or scanned.

It's tempting to fill business cards with information. The space is there, so why not use it? I've seen some business cards that would work well as billboards, because they contain too much information for the eye to readily absorb.

The primary function of the business card is to identify who you are, what you do, and how to find you. A good business card serves a second function, which is that you can write something on it when you mail or leave it. For example, you could write your cell number, or "Sorry I missed you," or "Thanks!" For this reason, I recommend that you don't emboss anything on your business cards because then the back of the card won't be a flat surface on which you can easily jot a few words. For the same reason, don't print a solid color on the back of your business card and don't fill both sides with information that squeezes out the room to write.

If you feel compelled to use your business card as a compendium of printed data, get business cards with a gate or foldover, and then leave one of the foldover panels blank so that you can use it as note space.

For longer letters you will need a supply of second sheets for the pages other than the first page. Second sheets can be plain paper (the same paper as for your letterhead, but unprinted) or sheets that have the name of your practice printed at the top or the bottom. One reason to use matching paper is that your clients will look to you to keep track of the details of their transactions and disputes, and if you use mismatched paper, then you are conveying the impression that you don't notice details.

If you decide on simple and understated letterhead, then you can have your letterhead and cards engraved. Engraving produces an attractive result but is more expensive than offset printing. If you want to display a logotype or emblem on your cards and letterhead, or if you want to use a splotch of color, then you will get a better result from offset printing.

Your printer may suggest using thermography to print your cards and letterhead, because it is cheaper than engraving. Thermography produces a raised-type effect similar to engraving, and for that reason has a reputation, sometimes deserved, of being a bad imitation of engraving rather than a printing method with its own strong and weak points.

Besides your letterhead, obtain some note cards on which you can write letters to clients that are too long to fit on a business card but informal enough not to be printed on your letterhead. I use note cards with the firm name and website address as thank-you notes. If you get notecards and matching envelopes, choose a size that can be mailed at standard letter rates. If you don't, then you or your assistant will need to remember to put nonstandard (extra) postage on your notecards or else the Postal Service will return your notecards for additional postage due.

Currently (2014) to be mailed at standard letter rates, an envelope must be rectangular, be between 3.5 and 6.125 inches high and between 5 and 11.5 inches long, and have an aspect ratio (length divided by height) between 1.3 and 2.5. If your notecard envelopes are 4.625 inches high (as our firm's A2 notecard envelopes are), then to be mailed at standard postage they must be more than 6 inches long (6.0125 inches to be exact). We didn't think of the extra postage when we selected our notecards, and we ordered notecards sized for A2 envelopes. A2 envelopes are very common for announcements, but they are only 5.625 inches long and have an aspect ratio that is less than 1.3, so they require extra postage to mail. The slightly larger A6 size (4.75 by 6.5 inches) is a better choice for your notecard envelopes as they can be mailed with standard postage.

B. Your Office on the Internet

Whether your office is high in a tower or in a suburban storefront at street level or in your spare bedroom at home, you have a second office location, which is your virtual presence on the Internet. Prospective clients who in past decades might have seen your office or your sign while walking around town, or who might have paged through a telephone directory to find a lawyer, now do their walking and paging through their computers. They will get an impression of your practice and decide whether to call you based on your Internet presence, just as in past years a client might have looked in your office window before deciding whether to open your door.

1. Your Website Has Replaced Your Listing in the Telephone Book

Back when the telephone company printed and distributed telephone books, the books had two sections, and in larger cities two volumes. The White Pages listed every subscriber and business alphabetically. The Yellow Pages listed businesses by category, and then alphabetically within each category. The two sections served two different purposes. If you knew who you were looking for and wanted to call or write to this individual, you could find his or her address and telephone number in the White Pages. If you were looking for a particular type of business, you would go to that category in the Yellow Pages and read the listings and advertisements until you found one that you wished to call. So if you knew that you wanted to call me, you would look for my name in the White Pages, or possibly for my name and number in the Yellow Pages under "Attorneys." If you were looking for an attorney but had no particular attorney in mind, you would go to the Yellow Pages and look through the listings under "Attorneys" until you found the name of an attorney you recognized or one in your part of town or one whose advertisement you noticed.

The Web has made the White Pages and Yellow Pages nearly obsolete, and telephone books are passing into history. (When was the last time you opened one?) But your website will serve the same function that the White Pages served. Depending on your business plan, your website may also replace the advertisement you might have put in the Yellow Pages.

Your website replaces the White Pages because it's how people who are looking for you in particular will find your address and telephone number. Twenty years ago they would have looked you up in the alphabetical directory; today they type your name into Google or Bing and find your website and contact information. If you do not have even the simplest of websites, then it's as if you weren't listed in the White Pages. Don't make it hard for clients who are looking for you in particular to find you. Even a one-page website that merely states who you are, where you are, and what you do will get your name and telephone number into the equivalent of the White Pages.

How about the Yellow Pages? If you want to get business through the Internet, meaning from people who are looking for a real estate lawyer in your area or with your experience, but who don't know who you are yet and who aren't searching for you by name, then your website will need a lot more heft so that search engines will find it and rank it on the first page of search results. These prospective clients are not searching for you specifically—they are not using search terms such as "Dean Alterman" and "lawyer" to find you. They are using much broader search terms, perhaps something like "real estate lawyer" and "Portland, Oregon," which may yield several million search results, somewhere among which might be your website.[1] Your website will need to stand out, not from websites of other lawyers whose names resemble yours, but from those of other lawyers who are in your city and practice area. Because your prospective clients will be searching not for you but for particular keywords (search terms), your website designer will have to include both visible and invisible keywords to identify your site to the leading search engines to increase the chance that a link to your site will appear on the first page of search results.[2] If your designer does not understand search engine optimization, often called simply SEO, then you will need some assistance from an expert in SEO to choose keywords and descriptors that will make it more likely that Google and Bing will rank your site higher instead of lower.

If you are building a "Yellow Pages" site to attract new business, once you have your site showing up well in search results, you will need to have enough content on your site to persuade prospective clients that you're the right lawyer for them to call about their matter. Some clients will be attracted by your description of other matters you've handled. If your website says that you've handled 200 property tax appeals, someone looking for a property tax lawyer is more likely to find your website and to become

---

1. The difference in results is huge between a White Pages-type search for a specific lawyer and a Yellow Pages-type search for a lawyer who practices in a particular field. A search for "Dean Alterman," "lawyer," and "Portland" produced 3,070 results. A search for "real estate lawyer" and "Portland" produced 65,900 results. A search for the phrase "real estate lawyer Portland," not enclosed in quotation marks, produced 2,690,000 results. A search for "real estate attorney Portland," also without quotation marks, produced 3,620,000 results.
2. A 2011 study of 8 million Google clicks by Chitika, a consultancy, reported that only 6 percent of the searchers clicked through to the second page of search results.

your 201st property tax appeal. If your website describes three or four commercial transactions you've handled, a prospect with a similar commercial transaction who finds that page is more likely to call you to handle that transaction.

Other clients may be looking not for specialized knowledge but for price or convenience. If your business plan is to compete on convenience, then your website should say why it will be convenient to hire you. Perhaps you offer evening appointments, or you validate parking, or you make house calls. Make your website fit your business plan.

2. Your E-Mail Doesn't Just Receive Messages; It Sends a Message Also

Another part of your electronic presence is your choice of e-mail. Domain names are cheap. Get a domain name for your website that includes either your name or your practice area, and then get an e-mail address that matches your domain name. Don't put your website on someone else's domain name, and don't use someone else's domain name for your e-mail.

If you use a free domain for your business e-mail (e.g., @hotmail.com, @gmail.com, @aol.com, or @yahoo.com) then you are making at least four mistakes. The first is that you are sending a poor marketing message to your clients and contacts by implying that you don't really have a business of your own. The second is that you're letting them infer that their e-mail messages to you aren't confidential. The third is that you're risking the chance that a corporate reorganization will force you to change your e-mail address and get in the way of your clients reaching you.[3] The fourth is that you are missing a chance to advertise yourself and your practice. An e-mail message to your client from "janedoe@janedoelawyer.com" publicizes who you are and what you do in a way that a message from "janedoe@yahoo.com" doesn't.

---

3. This situation happened to my family for our home e-mail when Verizon sold its local telephone business to Frontier and hundreds of thousands of subscribers had to change their e-mail domain from verizon.com to frontier.net, which meant not just notifying our friends but changing our login information on several dozen websites we use and our contact information with schools and businesses.

C. The Right Equipment

You will need a computer, two printers (because one will break the morning that your largest client is closing a sale), and Internet and e-mail access. Everyone on your staff will need a computer also. Buy machines that are all the same and that run the same software. You will also need a server to connect the machines in your office to each other, to the outside world through e-mail and the Internet, and to your printer/scanner. The trend is for computers to send and receive more data, so buy a server that is more powerful than you need. Buy for tomorrow's needs, not today's.

I recommend starting out with a workhorse black-and-white printer and having at least a lightweight color printer. The black-and-white printer will cover most of your needs, but not all—and particularly not when it comes to maps. You will find yourself wanting to print and keep zoning maps, satellite photos, shots from Google Earth, and other sources where color is essential. Most of our local jurisdictions publish their zoning maps online, in color. If you print a zoning map in black and white, and don't hand-color it in immediately (a tedious and error-prone task), you will look back on the map two weeks later and not be able to tell the difference between orange cross-hatching (general commercial zoning, perhaps) and yellow cross-hatching (low-density commercial, perhaps)—the orange zoning and the yellow zoning will look the same in black and white.

Similarly, a city's utility maps may show water, sanitary sewer, storm sewer, and other lines all on one map, in different colors. Your clients, who may not know that the maps are available, will appreciate your sending them utility maps for their property, but only if they can tell the sanitary sewer apart from the storm sewer. You can't see the difference in black and white; you can in color. As I write, you can buy a lightweight color printer for about $300. Each page is expensive to print, but then you're not going to print a lot of color pages.

Unless you don't edit documents on screen (and few of us don't), get two large monitors instead of one small monitor. With two monitors, you can put a reference document on one screen and the document you're editing on the other, without having to squeeze the windows for two documents into one small screen. You can also separate the screens by function, using one for e-mail and timekeeping and the other for word processing.

A modern office telephone has programmable buttons. Two functions to insist that your system will support are conference calling (being able to join two calls together) and do-not-disturb (DND). Services such as freeconferencecall.com are available to handle large prearranged conference calls, but you'll often be talking on the phone with a client when a question comes up for which you'd like to have another person (an escrow officer, a lender, a consultant) on the phone for a three-way conference. The conference call function lets you do that at your telephone. The DND function mutes the ringtone on your phone. An incoming call will still flash, but it won't sound. If you have voice mail native to your phone system, when you turn DND on, your incoming calls will flash once or twice and then go directly to your mailbox. The DND function will allow you to focus on one task without being interrupted by the ringtones. And you can use the DND function as a sales tool: you send a powerful message to a client who is meeting you in your office if the first thing you say is "Let me turn off my telephone so that we won't be interrupted," and then you press the DND button to silence your phone.

If you will have a separate conference room, invest in a good-quality full-duplex speakerphone. Some speakerphones are half-duplex, meaning that they can transmit sound in only one direction at a time. If you are using a half-duplex speakerphone in your conference room, then whenever someone in your room is talking, you won't be able to hear what the other people on the conference call are saying. A little noise in your conference room, perhaps even the clatter of a coffee cup on a coaster, will blank out the voices of the other callers. By contrast, a full-duplex speakerphone can transmit sound in both directions at the same time. Noises in your office won't cut off the other callers.

Whether or not you will have a separate conference room, get a speakerphone function for the telephone in your office. You will sometimes want to have a client with you when you call opposing counsel. You will also have occasions to be a silent participant on a long conference call, for which it's very convenient to be able to leave the speaker on, mute your microphone, and listen to the call without having to worry about conversations in your office being piped to the other participants.

D. To Fax or Not to Fax

To lawyers my age and older, the fax is new technology, but it's actually older than the telephone. The first facsimile machine was invented in 1843 and could send an image over a telegraph wire. (The telephone would not be invented for another 33 years.) The technology improved in fits and starts, and the fax machines of the 1960s could send a letter-sized document over a telephone line in about six minutes. Fax machines didn't become widespread in law offices until the 1980s, and the ring of the fax machine meant that an important document was about to arrive. The fax machine became an efficient way to send an image.

Thirty years later, the office fax machine is nearly silent, supplanted by e-mail. E-mail is a faster way to send an image, and e-mail can carry an editable document as an attachment, which the fax machine can't do. Machines that used to ring dozens of times a day now receive a few messages a month. Unless you do business with clients who are in those rare places abroad where faxes are common but e-mail is rare, or unless you regularly file documents with a court or agency that will accept faxed documents but not e-mailed documents, you can do without a separate fax machine.

Instead of buying a fax machine that will quietly gather dust, buy a scanner that can convert your documents to PDF images that you can then save in your electronic filing system or annotate and e-mail to clients and counsel. A scanner will also allow you to scan incoming mail and save an electronic copy to your client file. If you scan your incoming mail and save it with meaningful file names or through good document management software that you use consistently, then when a client calls with a question about a document, instead of putting your client on hold while you search for the file, you can call up the document on your screen and answer the client's question directly. You can do without a stand-alone scanner if you buy or lease a copier that includes a scanner and that can be networked with your computer and server.

E. Software

Certain software is basic to most law practices: word processing, a spreadsheet program, and possibly a presentation program. Microsoft Office with PowerPoint covers these tasks, as do OpenOffice, developed by Sun Microsystems and now sponsored by The Apache Software Foundation, and LibreOffice, an offshoot of OpenOffice developed by The Document Foundation. Regardless of your choice of software, your word processor must be able to read and save documents in Word and PDF formats so that you can exchange documents with your colleagues and clients. WordPerfect, once the standard for law offices because of its user-friendly formatting and hassle-free automatic paragraph numbering, is now rare (maybe 2 percent of the documents I receive come in WPD format), but it's still useful to be able to read WordPerfect documents even if you choose Microsoft Word as your word processing program.

You will also want billing and accounting software. You will enter your time and fees into the billing software and use it to generate your invoices. You will also enter your income and expenses into the software to generate your financial reports.

You may want document management software—software that sits on top of your word processing program and indexes the documents you save. Until you get document management software, you will need to name and save your documents carefully so that you can find them again quickly without having to open dozens of computer files to find the one document for which you're searching.

Buy a spreadsheet program. You will receive and occasionally produce spreadsheets to be exhibits to leases and sales agreements. You can also set up a spreadsheet form to produce amortization tables for promissory notes. If you expect to read legal descriptions and you are adept in trigonometry, then set up a spreadsheet into which you can enter courses and bearings for metes and bounds legal descriptions and confirm that the descriptions close, meaning that the metes and bounds description ends up at the point whence it started. I set up some formulas in an Excel spreadsheet into which I can enter courses and distances from legal descriptions. The spreadsheet then converts each course into a coordinate (x, y) pair. If the final call ends up at (0, 0), then I know that the metes and bounds legal description closes. If the final call ends up at, for example, (100, 50) then I know that some errors lurk in the legal description. As a matter of routine I check metes and bounds descriptions that don't come directly from a surveyor. It occasionally happens that someone in years past retyped an old legal description and accidentally transposed two digits of a distance, or swapped "east" for "west," creating an error that later conveyancers perpetuated. I catch one of these errors every year or so.

If you are not confident about your trigonometric ability (or if the mathematics in the previous paragraph makes no sense to you), then consider buying software to plot and double-check metes and bounds legal descriptions. Software currently on the market includes DeedPro, Deed Plotter, Metes and Bounds, and many others. Programs are often advertised in *Probate & Property*, the magazine of the ABA's section of Real Property, Trust & Estate Law. Ask a surveyor for a recommendation.

Even if your accounting software comes with a budgeting function, you'll likely find it easier to do the budget for your practice on a spreadsheet. Once you have the form set up, you can use it to plan the finances of your practice, comparing your budgeted numbers to your actual income and expenses.

An aspect of software that is sometimes overlooked in a new office is arranging for regular backups of the data that your software produces. Back up your data at regular intervals, ideally every day but no less frequently than every week. There are several different ways to back up your data. One is to use a tape drive. You can attach a tape drive to your computer or server and copy the data sections of your hard drive to the tape drive every evening. If you back up your data with a tape drive, buy five tapes (one for each workday), label them with the day of use, and rotate them regularly. Tapes wear out. If you delegate to your assistant the task of doing the backups, check to make sure that the task is getting done. It's an easy task to set aside when it's already 4:55 in the afternoon.

Also, if you do use tapes, store them away from the office. Having a backup tape will protect you from loss if your computer crashes and destroys your hard drive, but it won't do you much good if it's sitting next to your computer when the sprinklers go off.

Because of the problems with making and storing tapes, many offices (ours included) are using outside services for regular backups. For a monthly fee, the outside service will access your server through the Internet nightly or weekly and download and store an encrypted copy of your server's hard drive.

You can also back up your data on a thumb drive or memory stick that you plug into your computer's USB port. As with the backup tapes, keep the memory stick somewhere away from your office so that if your computer is damaged or destroyed, you will still have the backup data.

Backing up your data regularly keeps your data secure against loss. You also need to keep it secure against theft and unauthorized copying and to protect your network against unauthorized access. If your network password is still "password" or "0000," put this book down now and change it to something more secure when you finish this paragraph. The breach of a list of 32 million passwords in 2009 allowed researchers to tally the most common passwords that users chose for their accounts. According to Imperva, a software company, the top four passwords on the list were "123456," "12345," "123456789," and "password."[4] Despite there being 32 million people in the studied pool, 20 percent of them (more than six million people) picked one of just 5,000 passwords. Choose passwords that are long but easy to remember, such as two unrelated words with a number or special character in between or at one end. You can remember a password that is (say) "sorrel24strife!" much more easily than you can recall "jxb!%42koo*."

Also, sophisticated clients are demanding that their lawyers implement and maintain security measures for their data. Banks and other lenders that you represent must comply with the Gramm-Leach-Bliley Act and the Federal Trade Commission's (FTC's) Safeguards Rule that implements the act. The act and the Safeguards Rule require financial institutions to safeguard sensitive financial information that they collect from their customers or keep in their files. Your law office is not a financial institution that the act and the rule cover directly, but your

---

4. Ashlee Vance, *If Your Password is 123456, Just Make It HackMe*, N.Y. TIMES, January 20, 2010.

lender clients are covered. If they send you financial information about their borrowers so that you can represent them in making and enforcing their loans, you will be a "service provider" as defined by the rule. The rule requires financial institutions to do two things with respect to their service providers:

- The financial institutions must take reasonable steps to select and retain service providers that can maintain adequate safeguards for the customer information that the financial institutions share with them; and
- The financial institutions must require their service providers by contract to implement and maintain the safeguards.

Even if you aren't going to represent financial institutions when you start your practice, if you want to attract business from lenders later on, you are going to have to implement and maintain adequate safeguards to protect the financial information on their customers that your lender clients will send you. If you don't, then the lenders can't do business with you. These requirements aren't new; Gramm-Leach-Bliley became law in 1999 and the FTC adopted the Safeguards Rule in 2001. They're only slowly penetrating to lawyers' practices, however.

F. Forms for Transactions and Forms for Your Practice Management

1. Preprinted Legal Forms

Does your county have a reputable publisher of legal forms? Get its catalog and read it. For many transactions, a preprinted form is adequate. You do not need to be embarrassed or abashed about presenting your client with a preprinted form as long as your client understands that you've used your legal training and experience to (a) select the correct form, and (b) complete it correctly.

The publisher's catalog will also give you ideas on how to organize your own forms library. Older practitioners (a category I'm entering) often keep forms in indexed notebooks: one section for residential leases, one section for office leases, one section for triple-net industrial leases, and so forth. If you also save your favorite agreements in electronic format, you can cut, paste, and edit much more efficiently than if you have to retype (or have retyped) long sections from one agreement to another.

Until you implement document management software, I recommend that you save your best forms in two different places on your computer: once in the client's electronic file and again in the forms file. When I started my own office, I set my server up to have a master folder for client documents, subfolders for each client, and subfolders within the client folders for each matter. Within the matter subfolders I have further subfolders for correspondence, pleadings, drafts, and other documents.

I also have a separate electronic forms folder, not tied to individual clients, which contains subfolders for practice areas: real estate, estate planning, probate, corporate, and so on. The real estate folder has subfolders for sales, leases, trust deeds, land sale contracts, and foreclosures. The sales subfolder has its own subfolders: earnest money agreements, escrow instructions, deeds, and so on. Several of the subfolders have subfolders for Oregon and Washington, the two states in which I'm licensed.

Other subfolders have clauses for specific problems. For example, I have one subfolder that contains different definitions of common area expenses and another with statutory disclosures. When I am writing a foreclosure letter and need to include a Fair Debt Collection Practices Act warning, I copy and paste the warning from the subfolder that contains statutory disclosures, editing it as necessary. You might have a folder in which you put the definitions of common area expenses from your leases, or different provisions for extension rights and options to purchase.

Through the forms folder, I can easily find (say) a triple-net multitenant lease for commercial property in Washington without recalling the client for whom I last wrote a triple-net multitenant commercial lease or the specific matter. In the electronic age that we inhabit, the real problem with information is not how to keep it, but how to index it so that you can find it again—how to find the document that you want from where it hides in the mass of information that you've accumulated.

2. Design and Construction Forms

For your developer clients, you can license the rights to use and modify the AIA (American Institute of Architects, http://www.aia.org) contract documents for a few hundred dollars a year, depending on how often you expect to use the forms. The AIA publishes more than 160 forms, which it divides into groups (the AIA calls them Families) based on how the project is being designed, built, and delivered. For example, the A201 Family of documents is suited for a project where the owner engages an architect to design the project and separately engages a contractor to build it under the supervision of the architect. The Design-Build Family of documents can handle a project where the other party both designs and builds the project. The Interiors Family is a set of documents for tenant improvement projects.

As you might expect, the AIA documents tend to favor the architects. The construction industry offers a competing set of forms that tend to favor the contractors. As an alternative to the AIA document families, or in addition to them, you can license the right to use the ConsensusDocs (http://www.consensusdocs.org), sponsored by a coalition that includes the Associated General Contractors of America, the National Subcontractors Alliance, and other trade groups from the construction, materials, equipment, and insurance industries. The ConsensusDocs are grouped similarly to the AIA's documents, including a series for general contracting, a series for design-build projects, and several others. Pricing is comparable to the AIA documents, with licenses available either for unlimited use for one year or for limited use of specific documents.

3. Your Own Forms

If you follow the advice I give you in Chapter XV about preparing forms that can easily be adapted to other transactions, then from time to time you'll create forms you really like. It's a simple matter at the end of the transaction to adapt that form to be generic—to take out the identifying information for the particular client and transaction—and to add the form to your forms library. Start with a checklist of the forms you would really like to have. For a real estate practice, your list of forms could include residential and nonresidential mortgages and deeds of trust; statutory deeds; land sale contracts; purchase and sale agreements for houses, apartments, and commercial properties; and construction contracts. If you expect to handle leases, your list will also include leases for houses, apartments, single-tenant commercial or industrial buildings, and multitenant commercial or industrial buildings. Eventually you will write, or come across, a ground lease for a build-to-suit lease. Save those also.

When you remove the client-specific information from the form, also remove the metadata, the client-specific information that does not appear on your screen or in print but that is embedded in the file, so that the metadata relating to one client will not be included in the document that you send to another client.

As your practice grows, you will write other real estate documents that you can add to your forms library: access easements, utility easements, cotenancy agreements, eviction notices, letters of intent, and the list goes on. If you save these to your forms library as well as to the client folder, then when you're asked to prepare a utility easement, you can find your prior work easily and use it as a starting point without having to look up or remember the client and matter for which you last wrote one. Use a hierarchical structure for your computer forms library so that you can find your work easily. Here's a portion of a structure that you might use:

- Business formation
  - Corporations
  - LLCs
    - Articles of organization
    - Operating agreements
- Estate planning
  - Trust agreements
  - Wills
    - No trust
    - Credit shelter trust
    - Charitable trust
- Real estate
  - Financing
    - Mortgages

- Notes
- Deeds of trust
- Foreclosures
  - Oregon
    - Notice of default
    - Notice of sale
    - Advertisement
    - Affidavits
    - Trustee's deed
  - Washington
- Leases
  - Single tenant
  - Industrial multitenant
  - Office multitenant
    - Full-service
    - Triple-net
  - Retail
    - Percentage rent
  - Residential
- Purchases
  - Agreements
    - Apartments
    - Houses
    - Commercial
  - Deeds
    - Warranty
    - Bargain and sale
    - Quitclaim
  - Escrow instructions
  - Options

The important things about your file structure are that it should make sense to you (because you're going to be using it regularly) and that you can explain it to an associate or assistant who will be selecting forms from your forms library.

4. Government Forms

Does your state have a real estate transfer tax? Get the tax forms. If counties have their own individual forms without which they won't record deeds, get those, too. Those forms are usually free for the asking.

If you plan to handle house purchases and sales, get copies of the federal government's "Protect Your Family From Lead Paint in Your Home" brochure. Sellers (including your clients who may not have a broker) have to give buyers a copy of that pamphlet for most house sales, and you can save them the trouble by stocking copies in your office. As I write, my local publisher sells the government lead pamphlets for 50 cents each, so they are a small investment that will save your clients a lot of inconvenience.

Does your state have a seller-disclosure law? You should have copies of the seller-disclosure form, also as a convenience to your clients.

Fannie Mae and Freddie Mac publish standard single-family trust deeds for all 50 states. These are of only a little use for commercial transactions, but they are very good starting points if you need to prepare a trust deed for a single-family house. All of the state statutory language is in those forms. The agencies update them regularly and keep them current. Best of all for a new practitioner, they are available free! All you have to do is download them.

5. Real Estate Industry Sale and Lease Forms

Your state or local association of Realtors[5] will publish purchase and sale agreements and some standard addenda for use by their members. You can usually buy these forms (or license the right to use electronic copies) without being a member, or you can join as an affiliate member and become eligible to buy the forms.

For commercial transactions, your state or local Commercial Association of Realtors may publish forms for commercial leases and forms for commercial purchases and sales, available for use for a small charge. You can join your local Commercial Association of Realtors as an affiliate member and get access to the forms as well as an opportunity to expand your network.

---

5. The word "Realtor" is a trademark of the National Association of Realtors and is not a generic term for a real estate agent. As you will be dealing with other real estate professionals for many years, respect their trademark and capitalize it when you use it.

6. Your Internal Practice Management Forms
i. The Engagement Letter
Send every new client an engagement letter. You should develop a few standard forms for engagement letters that set out who the client is, what your engagement is, how you will charge for your services, and how and when the client will pay you. I discuss engagement letters in more depth in Section IX.B. A sample engagement letter with alternate clauses is included in Appendix 1.

ii. The New Matter Form
One of your most important forms is your new matter form, sometimes called a "new file form" or "matter opening form." Rather than leave file openings to chance, prepare and preprint new file and new matter forms with labeled blanks for the information that you should obtain whenever you take on a new client or a new matter. The form itself will serve as a checklist to remind you of what you need, and you can refer to the form in your first meeting or telephone call with a new client as a checklist to take down the basic information you will need to check for conflicts and begin the engagement.

A new matter form has some basic elements: the client's name and complete contact information, the name of the matter, a general description of the matter, the type of law involved, any known deadlines, the fee arrangement, and the adverse parties. The new matter form can hold a lot of other information. I've included a sample new matter form as Appendix 2.

Your new matter form should have enough room for you to write down every way that you can communicate with your client: a mailing address, a street address if the mailing address is a post office box or private mailbox, a telephone number, a fax number if the client has a fax, a cell phone number, and an e-mail address. If the client has a business phone and a home phone, get both numbers. Getting all available contact information will help you in two ways: first, if an emergency comes up you have several ways to try to reach your client. Second, if your client stops returning your calls and e-mails and vanishes, and you have to withdraw from representing the client, you at least have several different ways to send the message to the client that you have to withdraw. If you have to withdraw as litigation counsel, you will also be able to describe to the trial court your efforts to notify your client that you are withdrawing from the case.

iii. Checklists

A checklist is a simple and effective way to avoid serious errors. Airline pilots use preflight checklists to reduce the risk of accidents. Surgeons and nurses use checklists when operating on patients. In his 2009 book *The Checklist Manifesto*, Atul Gawande argues that as the responsibilities of professionals have become more complex, the professionals become more likely to miss something important in their work. Drawing on his own experience as a surgeon, Dr. Gawande suggests that more errors come from missing a step in a complicated process (that is, from forgetting to do something that we know we should do) than from not knowing how to carry out the process (i.e., from not knowing enough). The more procedural an assignment is, the more that a checklist can help the professional avoid an error of omission.

Your checklists will track both tasks and dates. The checklist is your list of the major tasks that you must do to complete the assignment, and it will also track the dates that they are due.

Bar associations and insurance carriers publish checklists to guide lawyers. One assignment well-suited for a checklist is a nonjudicial foreclosure of a trust deed. State statutes define a procedure with timelines and required steps, to which you can add the other steps you need to perform a foreclosure that complies with the law's requirements. A simple checklist for a foreclosure might look like this form.

Table VI-1: Foreclosure Checklist

Task	Date required	Date ordered/ started	Date received/ completed
Obtain loan documents			
Record appointment of successor trustee			
Order foreclosure guarantee			
Record notice of default			
Send notice of sale			

Task	Date required	Date ordered/ started	Date received/ completed
Order title update			
Advertise the sale			
Confirm lender's bid amount			
Order second title update			
Confirm no bankruptcy filing			
Conduct sale			
Record trustee's deed			

Your actual checklist would contain more information, such as the number of days required between the advertisement(s) and the sale date, and perhaps space to add notes about the title company from whom you order the foreclosure guarantee. If you have a checklist like this one in your foreclosure file, you have a simple way to avoid an embarrassing error, such as forgetting to place the advertisement for the sale or forgetting to comply with some other statutory requirement.

Residential evictions are also subject to stringent statutory requirements and are well-suited to checklists. Because even a small noncompliance with statutory requirements may compel a judge to dismiss an eviction proceeding, if you represent residential landlords in evictions, you will want a detailed checklist. For evictions, the checklist should include not just the steps that you expect to do as a lawyer (e.g., filing the complaint, serving the summons) but also the steps that your client may have done before engaging you (e.g., sending the notice of nonpayment, posting the notice of termination) and the documents that you need to get from your client before you file the case (e.g., the lease, the notice of nonpayment, the notice of termination, and any notices from the tenant about the condition of the apartment).

You can use checklists not just for assignments that are subject to strict statutory requirements, but also for assignments that have few statutory requirements but that follow a routine or that have contractual requirements. The checklist for the purchase of an apartment building might look like this chart.

Table VI-2: Sale-Purchase Checklist

Task	Date required	Date ordered/ started	Date received/ completed
Sale agreement signed			
Inspection completed			
Inspection condition satisfied or waived			
Loan application made			
Title report ordered			
Title objection letter			
Leases received			
Survey ordered/ received			
Survey approved			
Payoff letter from current lender			
Pro forma title policy			
Closing statement			

Keep the checklist in the file, but don't let it get lost amid the other papers. I will tag the checklist to be kept on top of the clipped papers on one side or the other of a folder insert, so that it is the first thing that I see when I open that insert.

iv. The Project List

An important part of managing your practice, though not exactly a form, is your project list. Your project list is not your to-do list, the list of tasks that you want to complete today. Your project list is a list of the active projects that you have on hand in the office. Mark Twain famously asserted that "the dullest pencil is better than the sharpest memory." Having a list of your active projects is a good way to ensure that none gets overlooked.

I suggest a simple project list, like this one, that you keep on your computer and update once a week.

Table VI-3: Project Status List

File	Status	Next task	Other info
101-5 Acme/Coyote	Lease draft sent to tenant 4/14	Revisions from tenant due 4/21	Still needs personal guaranty
119-1 Excelsior/WoodCo	Title report approved	Awaiting inspection approval, due 4/28	Additional earnest money deposited yet?
124-1 Fillmore/Pierce	Term expired 3/4	Appoint officers	

Instead of replacing the "status" entries each week with the new status, you can keep them in the table, so that your project list will also be a running log of your activity on all of your files. The project list will remind you of work that needs to be done.

G. Statutes and Reference Books

When I started practice in 1989, the firm that employed me bought each lawyer a complete set of state statutes every two years—that was the interval between the state's printed editions. One set cost as much as three hours of my billable time. As the price of the books rose, we cut back, and bought only the specific volumes that lawyers wanted for their practice area. I now buy my own volumes of the general civil code, the commercial laws, and the real estate and probate laws, statutes that cover 95 percent of my practice. For the other 5 percent, I can walk down the hall to get the library copy of the other volumes.

Today many states maintain their statutes online, where they're available free but with limited indexing. Private services such as Westlaw, LexisNexis, and CaseMaker also make statutes available for a fee, but with more indexing and cross references to cases.

My firm now buys one complete set of each edition of the Oregon statutes for our library (we still have a library) and individual books for each lawyer based on our practice areas. I have in my office three of the 15 state volumes: the volume on general practices including statutes of limitation; the volume on commercial law including the Uniform Commercial Code, corporations, partnerships, and limited liability companies; and the volume on real estate, probate, and trusts. These three volumes contain the statutes I most frequently consult.

I have two practical reasons for recommending to you that you buy hard copies of the real estate statutes of your state. The first is that if you meet with clients in a shared conference room instead of in your private office, you will occasionally have to consult state law while your clients are present. You can get the statute book and bring it to the conference room much more easily than you can bring your desktop computer to the conference room. The second is that if you search statutes only electronically, using key words, you will sometimes find a statute that seems to answer your question, and perhaps miss a statute that qualifies or limits the statute you found by an electronic search. When I consult my statute book and find a statute that I think applies to my problem, I read several pages before and after my statute to see the context in which the legislature put it. I sometimes find a statute that seems to answer my question, and then a page or two later I see another statute that begins with "Notwithstanding statute such-and-such, the following rule will apply." The word "notwithstanding" appears more than 40 times just in ORS 508, the chapter of Oregon law dealing with commercial fishing licenses. You can't find the "notwithstandings" so easily if you rely only on the electronic versions of the statutes.

If you will have a transactional practice, one important class of reference books for you to collect will be the manuals of policies and endorsements from your title insurers, which title companies will gladly give you in the hope that you will refer business to them. It's much easier to decide which title insurance endorsements your clients should request when you have in front of you the insurer's manual listing all of the endorsements that it offers in your state. Each insurer's manual will also state the insurer's requirements for issuing the particular endorsement and whether it's available for owner's policies, lender's policies, or both.

H. Your Paper Filing System

Despite the progress in electronic scanners and storage, and the advent of electronic filing of court documents and (in a few counties) electronic recording of deeds and mortgages, the paperless office is not quite with us. Lawyers continue to generate and receive original documents: deeds, mortgages and trust deeds, assignments, leases, promissory notes, and corporate minutes, and we continue to need to store and retrieve them. The main purpose of your filing system is not to store documents but to be able to find and retrieve them efficiently. Think about this fact for a moment. Consider a document that you file away and never need again. It makes no difference where you file it if you never want to look at it again. You could simply put it in a box with other assorted (and unsorted) documents or throw it away.

Our problem as lawyers is that when we store a document, we don't know for sure that we'll never need it again, so we have to file it where we can find it again without searching through hundreds or thousands of other documents. Our usual way to file client documents is in a file for the matter that the documents concern. We then have to arrange the files themselves so that we can find a particular file from the hundreds or thousands of files that we have in the office or in storage, and then arrange the documents in the file in a way that makes it easy to find the particular document that we want to consult.

1. Naming and Numbering Your Files

Let's start with designing a file-numbering system. The first requirement is that the system has to make sense to you. The second requirement is that the system has to make sense to your staff because you will be relying on your staff to place documents in the proper file and to find the proper file and documents when you need them again.

The design of your filing system will require several decisions: how you name and number your files, whether and how you name and save electronic copies, how you archive files, and how you store the papers themselves (manila folders, bucket files, notebooks).

First, let's look at the naming and numbering of your client files. In the simplest filing system, your files have no numbers, just client names.

Your files might have names like "Wiley Horner," "Augusta Solomon," and "Nathan Kief," in each case with a short description of the matter added. You can then store them alphabetically in the file room. The file number is simply the client name with a description of the matter, so the files for one client might be named "Nathan Kief—Alpha purchase," "Nathan Kief—Beta lease," and so on.

This system is simple but has two complications. One is that your billing software may not handle long file numbers. You may be forced to assign numbers or codes to your files simply to be able to enter your time and expenses and generate invoices. Another is that you may have more than one client with the same name. I once simultaneously represented, in unrelated matters, five unrelated people with the same last name. Three of them had the same first name. A file-naming system that relies on client names alone cannot handle a situation in which you have several clients with the same name.

A better system, and one that your billing software will encourage you to use, is to number your files. Some lawyers number their files in consecutive order: file no. 101 is the lawyer's first matter, no. 102 is the second matter, no. 103 is the third matter, and so on. One variant of this numbering system is to number the files by year opened: the first matter in 2015 is 2015-1, the second matter is 2015-2, and so on.

This system can work well for an office that doesn't get repeat business—where almost every client brings in one matter and one matter only. If you expect repeat business, then you should not use a system in which the files are numbered 1, 2, 3, and so on, because it will result in the files for one client being scattered. A client who brings you three matters a year may have files numbered 2014-4, 2014-15, 2014-22, 2015-1, 2015-11, and 2015-20. Those six files will be in six different places in your file room. That's inefficient if they relate to the same property (i.e., if they are six different leases for the same building). It's also inefficient if you need to find a particular document or if you need to assemble all the files for copying or to be transferred to another law office.

I strongly suggest that you use client and matter numbers, and not just matter numbers. Your first client can be client no. 101 and that client's first matter can be matter 1. The file number for that matter would be 101-1.

The client's second matter would be no. 101-2, the third matter would be 101-3, and so on. All the files for that client will be together on your shelf, and easy to find.

Your next client would be client no. 102 and her first matter would be 102-1, her second matter would be 102-2, and so on.

You can use the concept of a client number followed by a matter number with a different numbering format to suit your preference, such as 101.001 and 101.002, or 101(1), 101(2), or 101-01, 101-02. If you form corporations for your clients, consider reserving matter no. 1 for general advice to the client and matter no. 2 for the corporate minutes and other documents relating to keeping the corporation in good standing. The first specific matter for the corporation would then be matter no. 3. So if a client asks you to form a corporation and prepare the organizational documents, you would then open files numbered (say) 256-01 for future general advice and 256-02 for the corporate organization. If the client brought you a real estate purchase, you would open file 256-03 for that purchase.

A variant of this system is to use a letter for the client's last name or company name as part of the file number, so your first client whose name begins with "A" would have matters numbered A101-1, A101-2, and so on.

As real estate investors acquire more and larger properties, they will start to form entities (usually limited liability companies but sometimes partnerships) in which to hold their investments. For filing purposes, you may index the related entities under the name of the principal, opening separate matters under one client name and number. For instance, your client Cantor may have several affiliates, perhaps Cantor Aleph LLC, Cantor Beth LLC, Cantor Gimel LLC, and so on. Let's say that Cantor's client number is 110. Your general Cantor file may be 110-1. Then Cantor brings you a lease in Cantor Aleph's property, so you open file no. 110-2, labeling it "Cantor Aleph/Acme Catering lease." As you open more files for Cantor and its subsidiaries, it may end up that files nos. 110-2, 110-7, and 110-9 are for Cantor Aleph, files nos. 110-3, 110-4, and 110-8 are for Cantor Beth, file no. 110-6 is for Cantor Gimel, and the other files in your 110 series are for the parent companies.

Then one day you notice that in accordance with the special-purpose entity requirements of his loan agreements, Cantor is paying your fees from an assortment of checking accounts: one for Cantor, another for Cantor Aleph, a third for Cantor Beth, and a fourth for Cantor Gimel. Cantor or Cantor's bookkeeper is likely going through some effort to sort out your invoices to allocate them to the proper entities. Your file numbering, simple for you, is causing extra work for your client. Yet if you give each of the Cantor entities separate file numbers, the Cantor files will be scattered in different places in your file room. The potential for confusion can become infinite.

When I take on a client with several entities, or one that I expect will do business through several entities, my solution is to reserve a block of client numbers for that client's partnerships and companies as soon as I figure out that I may need them for that client. I will also skip some client numbers and assign the parent company a file number ending in 00. So, for example, if Cantor hired me to represent Cantor and its affiliates, I might assign Cantor the client number 7100 and then reserve the next 9 (or maybe the next 29 or 49 or 99) numbers for affiliates of Cantor.

Because I will give all the Cantor entities consecutive client numbers, all of the Cantor files will be together. Because each entity has its own client number, all of the files for each entity will be together also. The file for Cantor Aleph, matter 1 will be next to the file for Cantor Aleph, matter 2, with nothing in between.

2. Physically Making Your Files

Now that you have decided how you will name and number your files, decide how you will physically make them—what they will look like and how you will sort the papers within the file.

The simplest storage method is the plain manila folder. You can buy manila folders that have prongs for two-hole punched paper preinserted. Use the prongs to hold papers so that they don't fall out. Choose folders with side tabs, not top tabs, so that you can store them in a side-loading file cabinet and get to them without pulling out a drawer. Put stick-on numbers on the side tab for indexing.

The advantages of using manila folders are that they are simple to label and easy to store. A file with only a few papers will take up a small amount of space on your shelf.

A larger file can be stored in what lawyers often call a "redwell," an expandable rectangular bucket made of thick reddish cardstock. It's actually a Redweld®, a brand name of All-State International, Inc., under which it markets several varieties of file folders and expandable files.[6] Within each Redweld bucket you place manila folders with the tabs on top to hold different categories of documents. For example, if I were opening a file for the purchase of a small shopping center, I would use a Redweld bucket that would then have separate manila folders for correspondence, the leases, the sale agreement, the title report and exceptions, the loan documents, and the other closing documents.

Redweld sells a useful accessory to the Redweld buckets, file handles made from Tyvek®, called Color-Bands®. You can print a file name and file number on the Color-Bands by hand or through a printer, and then attach the Color-Band to the Redweld bucket as a sort of pull handle. The Color-Bands come in 26 different colors. You can assign one to each letter of the alphabet and use the color coding to indicate the client, or you can use the colors to indicate the year that the file was opened, or you can use the colors to indicate which attorney in the office is responsible for the file. Because they're made from Tyvek the Color-Bands are quite durable.

Manila folders also come in different colors, and you can code the contents of a Redweld bucket by using inserts of different colors. If you regularly handle purchases and sales, you might standardize the inserts by using a green manila folder for loan documents, a red folder for the title report, and a blue folder for the purchase and sale agreement. Use the special colors for the documents you'll most often need to refer to. A title report is easy to find if it's always in the red subfolder, but not so easy if it's punched and inserted with correspondence in a single large file.

Some lawyers prefer to keep their files in three-ring binders. Most papers are punched and placed in the binders, which then can stand upright on the shelf. Within the binders, index tabs are used to sort the different documents by type or class. One advantage of using three-ring binders is that the documents tend to stay in place. A document attached by three rings

---

6.   The products are available through http://www.redweld.com and many office products dealers.

is more likely to stay in place than one attached to a manila folder by two prongs. One disadvantage is that the three-ring binders take up a lot of space whether they're full or not. If they're of good quality they are also more expensive than manila folders and Redweld buckets.

You can save some space and some money by using manila folders for files that will hold only a few papers and using Redweld buckets for files that will have more papers. I do suggest using a Redweld bucket for any file that will hold an original document, such as a lease, because you can insert the original lease into a color-coded insert so that it will stand out in the bucket file. If you use one manila folder to hold all the papers in a file, then the original document (or its equivalent, your copy of the signed lease, for instance) will end up somewhere in the middle of the file, and you will have to thumb through the file when you want to refer to it.

Make the documents that you're most likely to want to refer to again the easiest ones to find. Two years after you've negotiated and drafted a lease, you probably won't need to reread the correspondence between you and the tenant's lawyer about whether the parties should be "landlord" and "tenant" or "lessor" and "lessee," but you may need to reread provisions of the lease in order to answer a question from your client about a late payment or a change of use or a request to consent to an assignment or subletting. Don't let those documents get buried amid others in a single bulky stack; make a separate subfolder for final documents such as a signed lease.

Chapter VII

Staffing Your Office

A. What Is to Be Done and Should You Do It?

One of your first decisions in planning your office will be to determine what staffing you will need.

Two kinds of tasks should be delegated to your staff or outsourced to others. Delegate or outsource tasks that don't require your legal knowledge and tasks that you don't know how to do. The reason you should hire someone to do the tasks that don't require your legal knowledge is so that you can devote your time to giving legal advice to your clients. The reason to hire someone to do the tasks that you don't know how to do is because they will do those tasks better and more cheaply than you will. In both cases, your goal is to free up your time from being absorbed by those tasks that don't need you so that you can focus on the work that your clients are hiring you to accomplish.

1. Delegate What You Can: The Tasks That Don't Need You

The first group of tasks include both the mundane and the complex, with the more complex of the group edging into the second group of tasks. For example, one mundane task in the first group is to prepare and send certified mail. The process is nitpicky: Find a certified-mail sticker, insert the number on the sticker into the letter that you're mailing, fill out the receipt card, attach the sticker and the card to the envelope, and either take the letter to the post office to pay the postage, or print a postage sticker on your postage meter.[1] You can take twenty minutes to prepare and send the envelope with the sticker and the receipt card, or you can use the twenty minutes to return phone calls and e-mails from clients while your assistant prepares and sends the envelope in ten minutes.

Another mundane task is opening, stamping, and processing mail. You can process the mail yourself, or you can have an assistant process the mail and then bring today's mail to your desk, each piece now bearing your office's "Received" stamp and clipped to the appropriate file. Identify the office duties that take you away from practicing law, and hire someone to do them for you. Even if you start your practice with only a few clients who do not keep you busy for the full day, you can hire and pay a part-time assistant to take over these office duties for you. The cost of $50 or $100/day to have an assistant is cheap if your assistant frees you to do another $300 of work for your clients.

You can outsource some tasks in the first group. For example, if you offer coffee and tea to your clients and drink coffee or tea during the workday yourself, you can make weekend runs to the store to stock the office, or have your assistant take part of the workday to buy coffee and tea. As an alternative, you can contract with a coffee service company to install a coffee maker and bring supplies of coffee and tea so that neither you nor your assistant need to leave the office for this errand. You can buy your own coffee and tea more cheaply than the coffee service can provide it only if you value your time at zero.

2. Delegate What You Must: The Tasks You Can't Do

Recognize the tasks in the second group also, those tasks that you should not do yourself because someone else can do them much better than you can. These can include managing and running your billing system, supervising your computer equipment and Internet connection, and preparing your business tax returns. You can learn how to keep your own books and prepare your business tax returns, or you can hire someone who already knows how. You can install your own software and hardware and troubleshoot

---

1. Sometimes there's an unexpected task, which is to print the postage sticker a second time when you notice that you forgot to change the amount of postage from regular first-class mail to the higher rate for certified mail, and then to find another envelope on which to use the sticker you printed with the wrong postage.

your computer network, or you can hire someone who already knows how. Bookkeepers and IT professionals are not clamoring to practice law; why should you take up bookkeeping as a hobby?

Similarly, you can manage and run your billing system, and print, fold, stamp, and mail your final bills each month, or you can hire a part-time employee who has some experience with your billing software to be your billing clerk. You will run your practice more efficiently if you delegate tasks that require expertise to people who already have that expertise.

B. Next, Assign Duties to Staff Positions

When I started my own office, I identified four staff positions that I needed to fill: receptionist, office manager, bookkeeper/billing clerk, and secretary. I also assigned the office tasks to these positions. My receptionist would greet visitors, answer the telephone, take messages, and handle coffee and tea service. My office manager would do all administrative work related to running the office, including buying office supplies, dealing with vendors, approving supply invoices for payment, placing service requests to the landlord, and handling my payroll service. My bookkeeper and billing clerk would prepare prebills, print and mail final bills to clients, enter invoices and expenses into the accounting system, and print financial statements for my tax accountant, my banker, and me. My secretary would process mail, handle filing, type letters, and manage the office calendar.

Four positions does not mean four employees. I filled the four positions with two people. One staffer was my secretary and receptionist, who handled the tasks of both jobs as a full-time employee. The other person was my office manager and billing clerk, who was a half-time employee.

If your model is to open a small office of your own rather than to rent a room in the office of another firm, then you will probably need one staff person. As the receptionist, he or she will welcome your clients when you are on the phone or in a meeting and politely deflect unwanted visitors. As your secretary, the same person will open, copy, scan, and file your incoming mail, enter appointments and reminders into your electronic calendar, and proofread and print your outgoing mail for you to sign. As your bookkeeper, the same person will enter income and expenses into your accounting software, prepare and print your prebills, print and mail your final bills, and prepare your financial statements.

If you type your own letters and are renting space in another office that provides a receptionist, your staffing needs may be low, perhaps a part-time person to copy and file your correspondence. If you are opening your practice in your own office suite, then you will want to have a receptionist, a secretary, and a bookkeeper. These don't have to be three different people. The same person may handle all three of these functions until you hire another lawyer. The important thing is to identify the support functions that you need and then to hire people to take care of them.

The right person can also be your legal assistant, helping you prepare documents for recording, obtaining title reports, doing first drafts of loan documents based on your office forms, and getting information from government agencies. If you handle purchases and sales, look for someone who has worked at a title insurer, escrow company, or real estate lender and will understand the lending and closing process.

C. Establish Employment Policies

If you have no employees at all, then you do not need to have any employment policies. But if you will have even one employee, then you should adopt at least a few employment policies to prevent misunderstandings between you and your staff. You should also adopt policies to state what you expect your employees to do. You should also adopt policies to carry out your ethical obligations. You do not need a 100-page employee handbook, but you do need to write down some basic employment policies and to discuss them with each new employee.

I suggest writing down at least your policies on hours of work, overtime, vacation time, sick leave or paid time off, and personal use of office computers. Your policy on working hours and days might look like this:

Regular office hours are from 8:30 to 5:00, Monday through Friday, legal holidays excepted. The office is closed from noon to 1:00 for lunch. The office is closed on New Year's Day, Martin Luther King Jr. Day, President's Day, Memorial Day, the Fourth of July, Labor Day, Thanksgiving Day, the Friday after Thanksgiving, and Christmas. If a holiday falls on a weekend then the office will be closed on the preceding Friday or following Monday, as observed by the federal government.

Your policy on overtime might look like this:

> The regular workweek includes 37.5 hours of work. Nonexempt employees who work more than 40 hours in a workweek will be paid time-and-a-half for the overtime hours in accordance with federal and state law. Employees may work overtime hours only with the approval of the supervising attorney.[2]

Adopt a policy that covers your employees' personal use of your office computers, network, and Internet connections. A policy of prohibition won't work—if there's an office of any size at which no one is connected to Facebook or eBay I have yet to hear of it. Your policy should reserve your right to control what software is installed on your computers, to limit Internet access if you need to conserve bandwidth,[3] and to state your right to read anything on the firm computers. Here's a policy that you might adopt for personal use of firm computers:

> The firm may inspect information on firm computers at any time, and no employee has any expectation of privacy in any data on a firm computer. The firm may restrict access to specific Internet sites and take other actions

---

2.   Even though you adopt this policy and tell your employees about it, an employee who works overtime hours without your approval is still entitled to be paid overtime for those hours. The Department of Labor makes this point clear in its regulations: "Work not requested but suffered or permitted is work time. For example, an employee may voluntarily continue to work at the end of the shift. He may be a pieceworker, he may desire to finish an assigned task or he may wish to correct errors, paste work tickets, and prepare time reports or other records. The reason is immaterial. The employer knows or has reason to believe that he is continuing to work and the time is working time." 29 C.F.R. § 785.11.
3.   Five coworkers who stream high-quality music at the same time can turn your Internet connection from allegro to lento.

as it deems appropriate. Employees should not use firm computers and e-mail accounts to transact outside business. Do not install software on your firm computer without the approval of [office manager] [partner].

Even if you adopt no other employment policies, you should adopt a policy to protect the confidentiality of client information, and you should discuss the policy with each of your employees. Model Rule of Professional Conduct (RPC) 1.6 obligates you to keep in confidence information that your clients give you. RPC 1.6(c) states: "A lawyer shall make reasonable efforts to prevent the inadvertent or unauthorized disclosure of, or unauthorized access to, information relating to the representation of a client." Comment 18 to RPC 1.6 elaborates on the rule:

> [18] Paragraph (c) requires a lawyer to act competently to safeguard information relating to the representation of a client against unauthorized access by third parties and against inadvertent or unauthorized disclosure by the lawyer or other persons who are participating in the representation of the client or who are subject to the lawyer's supervision. See Rules 1.1, 5.1 and 5.3. The unauthorized access to, or the inadvertent or unauthorized disclosure of, information relating to the representation of a client does not constitute a violation of paragraph (c) if the lawyer has made reasonable efforts to prevent the access or disclosure. Factors to be considered in determining the reasonableness of the lawyer's efforts include, but are not limited to, the sensitivity of the information, the likelihood of disclosure if additional safeguards are not employed, the cost of employing additional safeguards, the difficulty of implementing the safeguards, and the extent to which the safeguards adversely affect the lawyer's ability to represent clients (e.g., by making a device or important piece of software excessively difficult to use).

A lawyer's employees are "other persons who are * * * subject to the lawyer's supervision," and you must make reasonable efforts to prevent your staff from disclosing information relating to the representation of your clients. Your state bar may have a model policy on confidentiality. If not, here is a short policy statement that you can adopt:

All lawyers and staff at this firm owe a duty to the firm's clients to protect the confidentiality of their information. Do not share any information that you learn about our clients with anyone who is not employed by this firm, including your spouses and family members. Information about our clients that you think is "public knowledge" may include client confidences, and you may not discuss it with anyone outside the firm. An employee who violates our ethical obligation to keep in confidence information relating to our representation of our clients is subject to disciplinary action, including immediate termination.

I can't close this section without discussing the least important and most troublesome of the subjects on which you might adopt an office policy—whether to have a dress code. Some businesses adopt elaborate dress codes, and others get by without one. I opened my firm with a four-point dress code. The first point was the dress code of my high school, which I adopted verbatim; the second point was a longer form of my maxim "always be ready." The third and fourth points were as far as I dared to tread into the minefield of fashion.

- Dress should be neat and clean and appropriate to the task at hand.
- Lawyers must be able to see clients or appear in court without being embarrassed by what they are wearing.
- No visible ink.
- Do not wear blue jeans to the office.

When the firm expanded to have three partners, my views became a minority. We don't have a written dress code now, but we would all agree that the first point is our de facto standard. Proceed further at your own risk.

D. Obey the Fair Labor Standards Act and the Internal Revenue Code

The person you want to hire may ask you to pay him or her as an independent contractor and not as an employee, so that you won't withhold income tax and Social Security tax from the person's paycheck. Federal and state tax laws push employers to classify their staff as employees and not as independent contractors. If you and your staffer sign an agreement that states that your staffer is an independent contractor, he or she may become an independent contractor for some state law nontax purposes, such as liability for injuries and authority as your agent, but your staffer will not be treated as an independent contractor for tax purposes even though you have signed a contract that says so. Nor will your contract with the staffer exempt you from the Fair Labor Standards Act (FLSA), administered by the Department of Labor.

The FLSA protects employees, but not independent contractors. As with the Internal Revenue Service (IRS), the Department of Labor interprets the law to treat most workers as employees. The act itself defines "employ" as including "to suffer or permit to work," and (in the Department of Labor's words) to be "the broadest definition of employment under the law because it covers work that the employer directs or allows to take place." Independent contractors, the Department of Labor says, are "workers with economic independence who are in business for themselves." If you control the hours that your staffer works and your staffer works only for your practice, then your staffer is an employee under the FLSA.

The Internal Revenue Service also favors treating workers as employees and not as independent contractors, but to a slightly lesser degree. Current IRS guidance points to common-law rules and states the principle as follows: "The general rule is that an individual is an independent contractor if the payer has the right to control or direct only the result of the work and not what will be done and how it will be done." The IRS continues: "You are not an independent contractor if you perform services that can be controlled by an employer (what will be done and how it will be done). This applies even if you are given freedom of action. What matters is that the employer has the legal right to control the details of how the services are performed."[4]

If you succumb to a staffer's entreaties to be paid as an independent contractor and you are later audited by the IRS, you will be liable to

4. *Independent Contractor Defined*, IRS, http://www.irs.gov/Businesses/Small-Businesses-& -Self-Employed/Independent-Contractor-Defined, retrieved on June 15, 2014.

pay all of the employment taxes that you should have paid and to pay substantial penalties. Treat your employees as employees in accordance with the tax laws.

Chapter VIII

Finding Clients and Networking

A. Advertising for Clients

Lawyers advertise on radio, on television, in programs, on the Internet, on billboards, on bus benches, by direct mail, and in many other ways. You may not wish to advertise for clients, and if you are starting a new practice you may not have a budget to advertise for clients, but you must nevertheless market for practice. Even lawyers who disdain advertising as being beneath the dignity of the profession carry on marketing to locate new clients and to get more business from existing clients.

Our profession did not always allow advertising. When my father was admitted to the bar in 1950, lawyers could not advertise. Some lawyers believed it was unethical to hand out business cards. One bar association issued an opinion on whether a law firm could ethically display its name not just on a building directory but also on the floor directory. The tradition against lawyers advertising for business does not go back to the early days of the profession, but only to 1908, when the organized bar banned lawyer advertising. The ban on advertising lasted until 1977, when the United States Supreme Court in the case of *Bates v. State Bar of Arizona* announced that lawyer advertising was constitutionally protected commercial speech. States could regulate how lawyers advertised, but they could not prohibit lawyers from advertising.

Before 1908, some lawyers advertised. Abraham Lincoln advertised his law practice in the newspapers of Springfield, Illinois, until the year before he was elected president. Fifty years before Lincoln was admitted to the bar,

Samuel Johnson told his biographer James Boswell, who was a lawyer, that he would not solicit employment if he himself were a lawyer, "not because I should think it wrong, but because I should disdain it. However, I would not have a lawyer to be wanting to himself in using fair means. I would have him to inject a little hint now and then, to prevent his being overlooked."

One lawyer's "little hint now and then" is another lawyer's advertising. Whether or not you choose to advertise, you will need to drop some little hints now and then about who you are, what you do, and how you can be reached, if you expect clients to find their way to your door.

However you look for clients, you must comply with the rules of your state bar. Rule of Professional Conduct (RPC) 7.2 allows a lawyer to advertise services "through written, recorded or electronic communication, including public media." Any advertisement must include the name and office address of at least one lawyer or law firm responsible for its content.

RPC 7.2 regulates the content of advertisements and other solicitations. RPC 7.3 regulates who a lawyer may solicit for business. A lawyer cannot solicit professional employment for the lawyer's own profit in person, by telephone, or by real-time electronic contact unless the lawyer is contacting another lawyer, a family member, a person with whom the lawyer has a close personal relationship or a person with whom the lawyer has a prior professional relationship. This rule allows you to call your former clients and tell them that you are opening your own practice. You can also telephone and visit your family to say that you are opening your own practice.

RPC 7.3 does not prohibit you from renting a billboard. A billboard is not a "solicitation" under RPC 7.3 because it is not directed at a particular person. The official comment to RPC 7.3 says that a solicitation is "a targeted communication initiated by the lawyer that is directed to a specific person and that offers to provide, or can reasonably be understood as offering to provide, legal services. In contrast, a lawyer's communication typically does not constitute a solicitation if it is directed to the general public, such as through a billboard, an Internet banner advertisement, a website or a television commercial, or if it is in response to a request for information or is automatically generated in response to Internet searches."

RPC 7.3 is considerably less restrictive about what you can mail out. The rule requires you to include the words "Advertising Material" on the outside envelope of any written communication in which you solicit professional employment from someone known to be in need of legal services in a particular matter. This portion of RPC 7.3 does not apply to communications that you mail out to people you don't know to be in need of legal services in a particular matter. For example, you could mail an announcement of your new office location to accountants and real estate brokers in your area without printing "Advertising Material" on the envelope. You're not soliciting work from the accountants and real estate brokers for any particular matter, nor do you know them to be in need of legal services for a particular matter. You are simply letting them know that you are practicing law in their area.

B. Building Your Marketing Network

Unless you have a compelling marketing message, you will not fill your office simply from mailing out information about your practice. If you expect your clients to come from referrals as well as from direct contact—for example, if you are hoping that real estate brokers will refer clients to you—then you should get to know people who can refer business to you. You should also get to know people to whom you can refer your clients for the other work that they will need as they buy and sell real estate.

1. Real Estate Brokers
Someone who is buying or selling real estate will call a broker weeks or months before calling a lawyer. Brokers can be your best referral source. Get to know the local real estate brokers. You can meet brokers by offering to give speeches at real estate meetings or by writing articles on legal topics for newsletters of real estate organizations. Real estate offices are often willing to have lawyers come and talk to their agents about new developments in the law, new statutes, and new standard forms, especially if the lawyers' talks will count as credit hours toward the agents' continuing education requirements.

In all but the smallest towns, the brokerage industry is specialized. One group of agents will handle home sales only. Another group will handle sales and leasing of commercial and industrial properties. Within the commercial brokerages, the agents will often specialize, with one agent handling the firm's retail leasing and another handling apartment sales. If you are looking to focus on commercial real estate transactions, look for the agents in the commercial firms. One effective way to provide value to real estate agents is to speak about legal issues in the standard preprinted forms and to talk about how to write better custom clauses for those situations that the preprinted forms don't cover. For more than 20 years I have talked to real estate brokers about one small but important aspect of real estate agreements: how to write better contingencies. Each time I give the talk, I bring a one-page handout, an outline of the main points of my talk with enough blank space for the agents to take notes. I designed it to be easy for agents to keep—and it's on my office letterhead with my name, telephone number, and e-mail address.

I built much of my early practice on referrals from these talks. As I gained experience in more complex matters, I added talks on other topics for real estate agents, lenders, and lawyers, including

- Advising commercial tenants on small leases;
- What brokers need to know about planning and zoning;
- Permitted, prohibited, and exclusive use clauses in commercial leases;
- How the mortgage meltdown of 2009 happened (for this speech, I used props that included a white Panama hat, big sunglasses, gold-rimmed spectacles, and Monopoly deeds; it became a favorite);
- How to read a deed; and
- What the standard house sale form really says.

If you have a set of four or five short presentations on real estate law topics, the brokers will invite you to come to their sales meetings and speak, either directly or through the title insurance companies that are also working to keep their names in front of the brokers. The title insurance companies in my area are happy to sponsor these talks and to bring the doughnuts that provide an additional incentive for the brokers to attend.

2. Accountants

Not only do investors call their brokers before they call their lawyers, but when they're selling property, they often call their accountants first also. The American Institute of Certified Professional Accountants has state and local chapters that publish newsletters, in print or electronically, and that welcome articles about topics of interest to accountants. To emphasize your role as a real estate attorney, you can write and offer for publication an article about a tax issue that's important to real estate investors, but that accountants don't much deal with—property taxes and property tax appeals. A new property tax case from your state's tax court can provide the reason for writing the article, and an accountant who advises real estate investors may read it and pass it along to a client who has complained about his or her property tax assessment.

Accountants have different fields of practice, just as lawyers do. Some accountants do mainly tax work, preparing returns. Others do mainly audit work. Others provide specialized expertise in tax disputes and in tax planning. Some specialize in a specific industry; I knew an accountant whose particular field was auditing the gross sales figures of restaurants on behalf of landlords who wanted to verify that the tenants were paying all the percentage of rent to which the landlords were entitled.

When you hire an accountant to prepare your business taxes, look for an accountant whose clients include real estate investors, or whose clients include your clients.

3. Surveyors and Engineers

Property line disputes often originate because a landowner has hired a surveyor to stake property lines and mark property corners, only to discover that land within an old fenceline belongs to the neighbor. If you are willing to negotiate and litigate boundary disputes, then bring yourself to the attention of local surveying and engineering firms as a lawyer who can represent landowners in a property line dispute. When the surveyor reports that the fence isn't on the property line, the landowner's first question is often "do you know a lawyer who can help me?" Besides seeming to have the real estate history of the area at their fingertips, surveyors are also indispensable resources and (in my experience) fun people to work with.

Similarly, if you want to pursue a specialty in the environmental laws that affect real estate, get in touch with environmental engineering firms—the firms that produce the Phase I environmental reports that are a necessary part of all significant commercial real estate sales. You don't have to be the speaker or the writer on an environmental topic; the members of other professions have the same marketing needs that we do, and are also writing articles and giving speeches. Your local business newspaper will report on upcoming speeches and seminars; you can attend those and talk with the speakers, or call them, afterward.

4. Title and Escrow Companies

Not every real estate transaction involves lawyers and brokers, but almost every one involves a title insurer and a closing agent. Sales representatives of title companies will seek you out if you are advising real estate clients, hoping that you will refer business to them. Sometimes it works the other way around: One of my best clients came to me as a referral from an escrow officer who told him a few days before closing that one of the lender's requirements was that he take title through a limited liability company. His lawyer at the time was unavailable and he asked the escrow officer if she knew anyone who could form the company in 24 hours. She recommended me. I went on to handle nearly 60 other matters for him.

Even if your title insurer or escrow company does not become a source of business, its representatives can provide you with valuable information for your office: form books, underwriting manuals, the policies and endorsements that they issue, and lists of recent commercial transactions. Develop a good relationship with your local title company.

5. Lenders

One of the strongest desires of most real estate investors is to borrow money to buy more property or to refinance their holdings. From time to time, an investor will apply for a loan, obtain a loan commitment, and only then discover that the lender wants to lend to a single-purpose entity or obtain an opinion of borrower's counsel. If you become known for working promptly and effectively, then mortgage brokers will point their borrowers to you for that work.

If you choose your bank in part for its willingness to make real estate loans, then the loan officers to whom you refer your clients will refer other work to you. If you are regularly representing clients who borrow from your bank, and if you develop a reputation with the loan officers of being careful and prompt, they will refer borrowers to you when they get the chance.

If you bank at a community bank with traded stock, buy a few shares of the stock. You will receive the annual reports, be invited to the annual meeting of shareholders, and have an excuse to talk once or twice a year with the bank's management.

6. Other Lawyers

Referrals from other lawyers can be a good and steady source of business. Lawyer referrals fall into several categories, including

- Referrals from real estate lawyers who are too busy to take on a new client ("overflow work");
- Referrals from real estate lawyers who have a client conflict (one of their clients is buying property from another of their clients, and they can't represent both);
- Referrals from lawyers in other fields whose clients have a real estate need;
- Referrals from lawyers in other fields who have received a cold call from a prospective client with a real estate need; and
- Referrals from lawyers from another area whose clients have a real estate need in your community.

It sometimes happens that a lawyer will be asked to take on more work than he or she can handle at the time. In that situation, lawyers give priority to their regular clients and refer prospective clients (especially clients who aren't likely to become regular clients) to other lawyers who have the time to handle the matter. As you become more known as a real estate lawyer, you will occasionally get referrals from other real estate lawyers who are overbooked. Conversely, when prospective clients approach you to take on projects while you are fully booked, you can refer them to the real estate lawyers who are referring their overflow work to you.

More established lawyers with active real estate investors as clients will occasionally encounter situations in which one of their clients wants to buy or lease property from another, and they will have to refer one of their clients (sometimes both) to other counsel. If you receive a conflict referral of this sort, professional etiquette suggests that you not solicit other work from the referred client and that you keep in mind that the client's regular lawyer has referred the client to you to handle one transaction, not to take on as your own. The referring lawyer has sent you work that he or she was qualified to handle and would have handled but for the happenstance that the adverse party was also a client of that lawyer. The reason to not solicit other work from the referred client is not because of an ethical rule. It is a matter of professional courtesy. The custom is also followed for the practical reason that a lawyer who acquires a reputation as one who solicits more work from conflict referrals very soon won't get any more referrals from other lawyers.

No such custom exists for clients who are referred to you by lawyers who don't practice real estate law. The divorce attorney who refers a client to you for the sale of a house will not be offended if you later represent the same client in the purchase of another house because the referring attorney does not handle that type of work at all.

You can build your network of referrals among lawyers by cultivating solo and small firm practitioners who work in noncompeting fields. As you come into contact with other lawyers in your town, whether they be your classmates from law school or people you meet through bar association events, assemble a list of practitioners in divorce, personal injury, bankruptcy, immigration, intellectual property, and other fields outside of your practice area whose reputation is good. You will assemble your list so that when your clients and friends have legal needs that are outside your practice area, you will have at hand names and telephone numbers of lawyers to whom you can refer them. When you refer your client or friend to another lawyer, ask your client or friend for permission to tell the other lawyer about the referral. You can then send the lawyer a short note or e-mail along the lines of this: "One of my clients, John Smith, is looking for some legal advice about an auto accident that he was in last month, and I sent him your way. Let me know if he engages you." Even if your client or friend forgets to mention that you're the one who sent him to the other lawyer, the other lawyer will remember you and will be more likely to think of you when one of his or her clients needs a real estate lawyer.

Referral fees are more common in personal injury and other contingent fee work than they are in hourly and fixed-fee work. I have never asked for or accepted a referral fee in exchange for referring a client to another lawyer or law firm. Local custom varies, however, and if you do pay or receive a referral fee, be aware of the requirements of your jurisdiction's version of RPC 1.5(e). The rule states:

> (e) A division of a fee between lawyers who are not in the same firm may be made only if:
> (1) the division is in proportion to the services performed by each lawyer or each lawyer assumes joint responsibility for the representation;
> (2) the client agrees to the arrangement, including the share each lawyer will receive, and the agreement is confirmed in writing; and
> (3) the total fee is reasonable.

If you receive a referral fee from another lawyer, then either the fee must be in proportion to your respective shares of the work, or you must assume responsibility for the representation jointly with the other lawyer. Unless you are willing to assume professional responsibility for a project that is outside of your experience and your practice area, don't look for referral fees for hourly work that you send to other lawyers. Let the prospect of receiving client referrals back be reward enough.

C. Getting Your Name in Front of the Public

Some of your business will come from people referred to you by clients, and other business will come from people referred to you by members of your marketing network. Some clients will come to you directly because of your efforts to let your community know who you are, what you do, and where to find you.

1. Publish and Thrive

The section of Real Property, Trust and Estate Lawof the American Bar Association produces several printed and electronic publications. The editors are always looking for articles. Some are long and scholarly; some are short. Find an interesting topic and propose writing an article for publication. People whose work appears in print are more readily seen as being experts in their field. State and local bar associations also publish journals and magazines that need articles.

You can use a speech as the basis for an article, and you can use an article as a basis for a speech. To make your article last longer than the issue of the periodical in which it appears, order reprints of the article. The reprints provide a reason to be in touch with the members of your referral network. They also provide a reason to put your name before prospective clients and people who are not part of your referral network. For example, you might agree to write an article about insurance clauses in commercial leases. The fact that you're writing the article gives you a legitimate reason to call and meet with commercial insurance brokers to get their advice and thoughts, before you finish and publish the article. When your article appears, you can send reprints to the brokers whom you solicited for advice with handwritten notes of appreciation. You can also send reprints to leasing agents and commercial brokers, with a suitable cover letter, hoping that the recipient will find the information useful. Don't send a "Dear Broker" or "Dear Friend" letter; address each one by name.

2. Be Seen in Public

Nothing substitutes for person-to-person contact. Join a suitable real estate organization and attend the meetings. If you are active in the organization, you will soon be invited to join a committee, which gives you the opportunity to make contact with people in the real estate industry who may become referral sources for your practice. You can make a lot of contacts within your local Association of Realtors by volunteering to be on the forms committee and helping to write and revise the standard forms for selling and leasing property.

Join your state bar association's section of real estate law. Attend the meetings, and get to know the other lawyers who practice in our field. Whether or not they become referral sources, they will get to know you. When they find you on the opposite side of the transaction, you will be a known quantity and not simply a name and telephone number. Also, the section may present high-quality educational programs. You should attend them because you can network, advance your learning, and get continuing legal education (CLE) credits all at the same time.

Join the American Bar Association and the Section on Real Property, Trusts, and Estates (RPTE, pronounced "Rippity"). Every spring, RPTE produces and sponsors two days of CLE, joined to social events where real estate lawyers can meet others in the field.[1] As a member of RPTE, you will receive the Section's periodicals *Probate & Property* (a magazine devoted to publishing practical information on current topics and developments in real property, trust, and estate law) and *Real Property, Trust and Estate Law Journal* (a scholarly journal published in the form of a law review).

Most bar committees are looking for volunteers. To get the most out of your membership, sign up to join the real estate section, and volunteer to serve on the membership committee or the education committee. You will meet other practitioners more effectively as a contributing member of a small committee than as one of several hundred people in the audience at a seminar. Besides being a good way to add to your network and name familiarity, it's a way to give something back to your profession.

3. Let Your Clients Know That You Welcome Referrals

In my practice, most of my new clients come as referrals from existing clients. For what I do, the best way to obtain new clients is to provide outstanding service to my existing clients. Over time, more and more of the people who call you will tell you, "You come highly recommended by my good friend who is one of your clients."

---

1. You never know what professional opportunities might come to pass as a result of attending a section meeting. This book came about because I attended a RPTE meeting in Boston a few years ago, where I fell into conversation with a member of RPTE's publications committee.

Let your clients know, in a quiet way, that your practice is growing and that you're able to take on some additional work. Although I would not ask a client directly, "Whom do you know that is looking for a real estate lawyer?", I would hate to have my clients think that I wasn't interested in forming new client relationships and didn't want their referrals.

4. Join Community Groups and Nonprofits

One way to enhance your profile in your community is to serve on the board of a nonprofit organization or community group. Some organizations recruit their board members mainly for their ability to provide regular and substantial financial support, and nomination to those boards may be seen as a sign of having arrived socially, and thus something that people strive after.

For every nonprofit that can pick and choose among candidates clamoring to join its board, there are ten more (maybe 100 more) that must work hard to find competent trustees and volunteers. If you have the time and interest to help nonprofits, you will find many from which to choose with only a little effort.

You may decide to volunteer for a nonprofit for charitable or religious reasons or as a result of a friend's gentle persuasion. These are good reasons that are outside the scope of this book. I'm going to assume for this discussion that you are willing to donate your time and effort to a nonprofit organization from which you hope to increase your visibility in the community as well as attract some new business.

First, choose a solvent organization with a cause or mission that you support. You can get some basic financial information about a nonprofit by obtaining its Form 990s (its informational tax returns that it files with the Internal Revenue Service). Several services publish the Form 990s of nonprofits online.

Next, evaluate its board of trustees. Don't rely on the Form 990s for a current list of the board of trustees because the published ones are a few years old. Get the list of the current trustees from the organization's website or publications. Are the trustees all prominent people from out of state? It's not likely that you will be able to join the board.

A solvent local organization with local businesspeople and civic volunteers on its board, but with no lawyers, may be looking to augment its board with someone with the skills you have.

Before you commit to joining a board, ask about the time and financial commitment. Smaller nonprofits look to their board members to assist with fundraising and to be donors themselves. In our community, some organizations are known to expect $100 a year from their trustees, others expect to receive $1,000 a year from each trustee, and one or two expect most of their trustees to give $5,000 or $10,000 a year to the organization. Some organizations expect their trustees to commit time beyond the board and committee meetings, whether the time is in the form of soliciting donors for a capital campaign or flipping pancakes at a Sunday morning breakfast event. Know what you're signing up for before you sign up.

Chapter IX

Getting Hired: Initial Meetings and Engagement Letters

A. Initial Meetings—Do You Need Them?

Some prospective clients will want to meet you before they decide to engage you. Others will hope for a free meeting to get legal advice from you without having to pay for it. What your policy should be depends on your market area and your hunger for business. In general, I have found that people who expect to get your advice for free don't transition well to having to pay for it.

On the other hand, requiring prospective clients to come to your office for an initial meeting separates the people who are serious about hiring you from those who are simply hoping for a little free advice. Someone who is unwilling to make the effort to come to your office and meet with you in person may be unwilling to make the effort to pay you for your services or indeed to hire you at all. You may also want to meet prospective clients before you agree to represent them.

You may not need an initial meeting to take on a small project. If you are accepting an assignment that will take you one or two hours, it doesn't make sense to spend an additional hour meeting with the client. You may be able to get all the information you need by e-mail. Nor should you feel compelled to take several hours out of your day to travel to a client's distant location for a "beauty contest" interview to compete for a small assignment when you could be investing those hours in the clients that have already chosen to hire you.

For a larger project, the client will probably want to meet you first, for two reasons. One is that the client, particularly if he or she often hires lawyers, will want to get a sense of your experience and capacity to handle the client's situation. The other is that the client will want to decide if he or she can get along with you as an advisor.

For the same reason, I think it's a good idea for you to meet a prospective client first before you commit because you will be doing business with the client on this project for an extended period, and if the client's personality doesn't fit with yours, you should find out that you and the client aren't a good fit before you commit to taking the job. There are other reasons for you to want an initial meeting before you commit to taking the engagement. You may decide, once you've spent an hour with the prospective client, that he or she has an unrealistically high expectation of what you can do, or an unreasonably low expectation of what your fee and the associated costs will be.

B. Draft Strong Engagement Letters

Bar associations universally recommend that lawyers send engagement letters to their clients. A good engagement letter will clearly state several important things about the representation. First, it will identify the client. Is your client a person, both members of a couple, or an entity? You can get in trouble if an entity hires you to advise the entity, but the individuals in the entity think that you represent them also. As long as everyone is happy, no problems will occur, but if the entity and the individuals end up on opposite sides of a dispute, they will both be unhappy with you, and you may have to explain your thinking to the state bar.

Second, a good engagement letter will say what the engagement is for. What is the client hiring you to do? The engagement might be to advise on the purchase of a particular building, to prepare a lease for a particular tenant, to assist with a particular refinancing, to handle a particular piece of litigation, or to prepare an estate plan. If you are handling only part of a project (e.g., if you were advising on title issues with the purchase but not on tax issues), then your engagement letter needs to say that you are not giving advice on the tax issues. Otherwise, when the client is hit with an unexpected tax bill, the client will ask why you didn't give a warning.

Third, a good engagement letter will explain how you will charge for your services. It will state whether you are charging by the hour or by the project or as a fixed fee or with a guaranteed minimum and maximum fee or as a percentage or subject to a contingency. It will also state if you need to receive a deposit (sometimes called a retainer) from the client before you will start work, and how you will handle it. I will discuss deposits in Section XI.B as part of setting fees.

Fourth, a good engagement letter will explain what costs you pass on to the client. Do you charge for copies? Long-distance telephone calls? Delivery services? Postage? Recording fees? Dinner for staff and attorneys who have to work late?

Fifth, a good engagement letter will state how often you will bill your client. Do you intend to send bills monthly? Quarterly? Annually? When you complete the project? When you find the time to get around to sending bills? (I don't recommend this last choice.)

Sixth, a good engagement letter will explain what you will do if your client doesn't pay you on time. How far behind in paying you can the client be before you have the right to withdraw from representing the client? Your engagement letter should say that you can stop work if the client does not pay you.

Seventh, a good engagement letter will state how you will handle the client's file at the end of the engagement. The ethical rules of your state bar may require you to keep client files for a certain period of time, and it is a good idea to keep client files for several years, both for reference (because the client might call with a question about the matter) and to protect yourself in case the client later comes to believe that your work was inadequate. You are not, however, Iron Mountain, and you are not in the business of storing other people's files. The client should not expect to use your office as a private warehouse. Your engagement letter should give you the right to destroy the client's file after a certain number of years.

Eighth, a good engagement letter will reserve to you the right to withdraw from the representation if you decide you can't provide value to the client or if you are compelled to withdraw by the ethical rules of your state bar, if you and your client have a fundamental disagreement on strategy, or if the client asks you to do something illegal or unethical.

Your state bar may have sample engagement letters. Obtain a few, and study them carefully. Make it a practice to send an engagement letter to every new client. A sample engagement letter is included in Appendix 1.

Chapter X

How and When to Turn Down Work

A. Turning Down Clients and Engagements

You are not required to take on as a client every person who calls you or walks into your office, and you are not required to take on every new matter that your clients offer you. You may choose to turn down a matter for a substantive legal reason: perhaps you don't think the client has a good legal position, the statute of limitations may have run out on the client's claim, or the client may want to accomplish something that is illegal or fraudulent.

It's easy to turn down a matter if you don't think the client has a meritorious claim or defense. It can be more challenging to resist the temptation to take on a client with a good legal position, but sometimes you should. The matter may be outside your practice area. The client may need a lawyer to attend to it faster than your schedule will allow (e.g., the prospective client who brings you a claim today on which the statute of limitations will run the day after tomorrow). The client may be a lawyer shopper who flits from office to office with a shoebox full of papers, each time explaining why the client's current lawyer simply doesn't understand the facts of the matter. The client may expect more than a lawyer can offer: a large money award from a "hurt feelings" case or a six-inch dispute over a property line.

Let's talk first about whether you should take on a matter outside your practice area, a question answered both by the ethical rules and by good business management. Start with the ethical rules. Rule of Professional Conduct (RPC) 1.1 sets out the ethical rule:

Rule 1.1 Competence. A lawyer shall provide competent representation to a client. Competent representation requires the legal knowledge, skill, thoroughness and preparation reasonably necessary for the representation.

The comments to RPC 1.1 explain the rule further. The comments start with "A lawyer need not necessarily have special training or prior experience to handle legal problems of a type with which the lawyer is unfamiliar. Comment 2 also tells us that a newly admitted lawyer can be as competent as a practitioner with long experience." Whether you can provide competent representation depends on the legal problem. If you have some experience with leases and your state's landlord-tenant act but have never tried a case, you may be competent to represent a landlord in court in a residential eviction after you've spent a morning in landlord-tenant court watching other cases be heard. You can develop reasonable competence in the field, for a problem that requires that kind of work, with a little effort. As Comment 1 says, "In many instances, the required proficiency is that of a general practitioner." But even if you have 25 or 50 or 100 trial experiences in landlord-tenant court, you will likely agree that you don't have the legal knowledge to defend a capital murder case by yourself. Or, to use an example from real estate practice, you may have negotiated and prepared hundreds of leases and sale agreements but not be able to provide competent representation to a real estate syndicator on how to write an offering statement and comply with state and federal securities laws.

Note how the rule is phrased. The requirement is not that you be competent, but that you provide competent representation. For most of your work you will provide competent representation by having the necessary legal skills before you accept the engagement. The comments to RPC 1.1 allow you two other ways to provide competent representation if you do not have the necessary legal skills. One way is to study the field: "A lawyer can provide adequate representation in a wholly novel field through necessary study." If you have never negotiated an office lease, you may nevertheless be able to provide competent representation to an office tenant by acquiring the necessary legal skills through study. You can read treatises and CLE materials and do a short look through your state's recent case law to learn the basic principles and issues that often come up in drafting and negotiating office leases, or that lead to litigation when leases go wrong.

The other way is "through the association of a lawyer of established competence in the field in question." You can provide competent representation to a client in a new field by sharing the representation with a lawyer who is already competent in the field. For example, you may be fully competent to draft a will and trust agreement that will convey your client's assets to the people to whom the client wants to leave them, without knowing the intricacies of estate tax law or international estate planning. If your American client who is married to a foreign national and who has a taxable estate wants you to draw up an estate plan, you may consider yourself competent to draw up the documents that will carry out the client's wishes, but not to advise the client on the tax issues involved in leaving property to a citizen of another country. You can provide competent representation by associating with an estate planning lawyer who is familiar with those issues and who can design that portion of the client's estate plan, draft the appropriate language for the will and trust agreement, or review and edit your language and discuss with you and your client how American tax laws apply to bequests to foreign nationals.

To me, the important element of this example is that you are competent to do some of the work on the project and that you recognize what issues will require someone with experience in the field. If someone brings you a legal problem about which you know nothing but from which you might learn something useful in your practice, refer it to a lawyer who practices in the field, but stay involved with the project. For example, if you know nothing at all of estate planning and have never drawn a will, the client with the taxable estate and the foreign spouse is not the right client for you to do your first estate plan. It would be better to refer the client to an estate planning attorney with experience designing international estate plans. You can invite the client to have you review the plan, both so that you can confirm that it's consistent with what you know about the client's real estate holdings and so that you can learn a little about estate planning. Don't charge for the time you spend learning.

If the legal problem is something about which you know nothing and that has no relation at all to your practice and isn't in a field that you want to add to your practice, I suggest that you refer it to a lawyer who practices in the field rather than invest your time learning an unrelated field of law. One of your apartment owner clients is a tinkerer and amateur engineer who invents something, and asks you for help in obtaining a patent. Real estate clients have estate planning needs, but they don't usually have patent needs. You can learn something about patent law if you want to, but you won't be able to use that knowledge to help your other clients. Rather than study patent law and try to handle the matter yourself, refer your client to a patent attorney whose firm doesn't practice real estate law. The patent attorney will take care of your client far more efficiently than you could do yourself, and you won't have to spend hours of nonbillable time learning material that you can use only once or twice in your career. The patent attorney may have clients with real estate problems (inventors have houses also) and may refer their real estate work to you. Just as you don't want to learn how to prosecute a patent, the patent attorney doesn't want to learn how to negotiate an office lease or settle a boundary dispute.

You can quickly make the decision to accept or turn down work outside your main practice areas. A thornier problem is whether to accept or turn down work within your main practice areas. It's easy to turn down work that you don't know how to do, but it's much harder to turn down work that you can competently handle.

One clear reason to turn down an engagement is because you don't think the client has a good claim—you don't think that you can do anything to help the client. The prospective client wants you to collect rent from a tenant who moved out seven years ago and hasn't paid anything or acknowledged the debt since then, and the statute of limitations on a contract claim in your state is six years. You can explain to the client that the tenant can use the statute of limitations as a defense and then decline the case. As an alternative, you can tell the client that the client will lose in court if the tenant brings up the statute of limitations, but that you're willing to write a demand letter to the tenant for a small fee, in case the tenant pays some money or does something else that might revive the claim. Be clear in your engagement letter (see Sections VI.F.6 and IX.B for more on engagement letters) that you are promising only to write the demand letter and not to file suit. Consider asking for your fee up front. If you aren't clear with the client about the problem with the case, then you will write the demand letter, the tenant will consult a lawyer who will write you that the statute of limitations bars your client's claim, and your client will tell friends "Don't ever go to Lawyer X [you]. I hired X to collect some past due rent. X didn't recover a dime for me but still charged me hundreds of dollars just to write one letter." You don't need that sort of publicity or reputation in your community.

A second reason to turn down a matter that's within your practice area is if your time commitments won't allow you to handle it promptly. RPC 1.3 laconically sets out the standard:

> **Rule 1.3 Diligence.** A lawyer shall act with reasonable diligence and promptness in representing a client.

If a client offers you a matter that you can't handle in a reasonable time, or that has a deadline for action that conflicts with your existing commitments, you are better off to turn it down if you can't rearrange your other commitments not to conflict with the new matter. If you accept the matter anyway, you will make two clients unhappy: the new client, when you don't complete the matter on schedule, and the existing client whose work you push aside to handle the new matter.

What is a reasonable time in which to handle a client's matter? The business school answer would be that a reasonable time is whatever time makes the client happy with your service. If the client expects you to complete the project in three weeks and you complete it in two weeks, then the client will be satisfied with how quickly you completed the project. If the client expects you to complete the same project in one week and you take two weeks, the client will be unhappy.

As lawyers we will always rearrange our schedules to handle an emergency project for a good client. Don't feel obligated to rearrange your schedule to handle an emergency project for a prospective client if you'll have to break promises to your existing clients to do it. If you need two weeks to complete the offered project and the prospective client needs it in five days, turn it down and work on the projects that you already have on hand. Either the client will find another lawyer who will handle it in five days, or the client will reconsider and decide that two weeks would be fine.

B. Sending Nonengagement Letters

Nonengagement letters are almost as important as engagement letters. A prospective client may come to see you about a matter that you decide you don't want to take on (see Section X.C for more). Good practice is to send the prospective client a nonengagement letter—a letter stating that the person has not engaged you as his or her lawyer and that you have not agreed to take the person on as a client. Your nonengagement letter is especially important if the person has been sued and is under time pressure to file an answer, or if the person has a claim against another party and the statute of limitations is soon to expire. You do not want the prospective client thinking or saying that you had agreed to file an answer or handle the claim and to look to you or your insurance carrier for damages for having lost a default judgment or having a valid claim lapse.

Your nonengagement letter might read as follows:

Dear Mr. Nonclient:

Thank you for consulting me on March 5 about your dispute with Cora Friend over your common lot line. Having considered the facts you presented to me, I am declining your case and cannot represent you in this matter. Other attorneys may have a different view of the facts and the law than I do, and I encourage you to consult another attorney if you wish to pursue this matter. Property line claims such as yours are subject to statutes of limitation, meaning that you may lose the right to bring the claim if you do not file suit within X years after the encroachment started or became obvious.

I wish you the best with your claim and am sorry that I cannot take on your case.

Very truly yours,

Knott Engaged

Or, if you want to be less specific, you can write the following letter:

Dear Mr. Nonclient:

Thank you for consulting me on March 5 about your dispute with Cora Friend over your common lot line. Because of my other work commitments, I don't think that I could fairly represent you in this dispute, and I can't advise you or act as your lawyer in this matter. I encourage you to consult another attorney if you wish to pursue this claim. There is no charge for our March 5 meeting.

I wish you the best.

Very truly yours,

Knott Engaged

If you are turning down the project because you don't want to handle that type of engagement, you might send the following letter:

Dear Mr. Nonclient:

Thank you for consulting me on March 5 about your dispute with Cora Friend over your common lot line. Your lot line dispute is more complex than I am comfortable handling by myself and I recommend that you consult an attorney who regularly practices in this area so that you can get a better and more thorough evaluation of your case than I can give you. Although I can't take this matter on for you, I appreciate your considering me and would be happy to advise you on any real estate transactional matters that you might have in the future.

I wish you the best.

Very truly yours,

Knott Engaged

C. Recognizing Clients to Avoid

Watch out for the type of prospective client sometimes called the lawyer shopper.[1] The lawyer shopper is looking for a lawyer who will agree with his or her opinion of the law and (always poor) opinion of the lawyer shopper's current attorney. Often they will bring their case documents to your office in a shopping bag. Clients can have good reasons to switch lawyers once and sometimes twice, but the lawyer shopper switches lawyers every six or twelve months. If you take on a client who has been unhappy with and fired five lawyers in two years, and whose reason for switching lawyers is "my former lawyer simply didn't understand my case," a year later the client will have fired six lawyers in three years, you being the latest on the list. If your goal is to attract and retain long-term clients for your practice, then a client who can't maintain a long-term relationship with a lawyer isn't going to help your practice.

I'm less absolute about my next piece of advice, which is to avoid "hurt feelings" cases—matters where the legal fees are going to cost far more than the case is worth. In many instances, the best service you can render your client is to stress that the litigation is going to cost $25,000 and take a year or two to resolve, and to suggest the client will be happier spending the $25,000 on something more productive.

Beware of the client who tells you all about the relevant law, having picked it up on the Internet. It is your professional responsibility to understand and apply the law to the facts and not to take on a matter that is plainly without merit.

Also watch out for the client who wants to use you as an instrument of revenge, who wants you to make the opponent suffer and be miserable as a consequence of having mistreated your client. That sort of client will pester you for instant results, will barrage you with telephone calls and e-mails asking why the opponent isn't suffering yet, and will complain when you

---

1. The term "lawyer shopper" has been around for many years, meaning a client who switches from lawyer to lawyer, and is not related to the trademark "Lawyer Shopper," registered to Lawyer Shopper, LLC, of Phoenix, Arizona. No reference to the business of Lawyer Shopper, LLC, is intended and none should be implied.

charge for the time you spend answering your client's incessant e-mails and phone calls.

Chapter XI

Setting and Collecting Fees

A. Setting Your Fees

If you are entering real estate practice as part of a larger firm, then you may not have any choice in how to set fees. The firm management may have decreed that you must bill by the hour and may have set your hourly rate.

If, however, you are opening your own office, you have much more latitude in how to set fees. You can charge for your time (the traditional hourly rate), you can charge by the project (a fixed fee, possibly with milestones), or you can charge by the result (a contingent fee, the amount of which depends on the result you achieve for your client).

1. Hourly Rates
Despite the recurrent cries for the demise of the billable hour, most lawyers in business and real estate practice set their fees by counting the hours they work and multiplying by an hourly rate. When you set your hourly rate, you have to keep in mind several factors. One of them—not the most important—is how much you want to earn. If you have an income target, then you need to collect in fees all of the expenses for your practice plus as much money as you want to earn. How much you earn in a year is very important to you, but not at all important to your client. Your client does not care about your student loan payments or your home mortgage. Your client does care what the project will cost and when the client must pay you. As the accountants and business school professors say, "Cost is a fact.

Price is a policy." Your costs to run your office are facts, but the fees and rates that you charge are a policy that you are setting as a manager.

More important than your costs in setting your hourly rate is to figure out what the market is for lawyers in your area who do similar things. You cannot collaborate with lawyers outside your firm to fix prices (to charge the same fees) unless you want to gain first-hand experience with the Sherman Act as a defendant and be prosecuted for violating the federal antitrust statutes. You can, however, get information about the rates of other lawyers from different sources.

One easy source is fee petitions. Attorney fee petitions are a matter of public record. The fee petitions will name the attorney, the attorney's years of experience, and the attorney's hourly rate. Fee petitions are often filed in contract cases, in bankruptcies, and in divorce cases where one partner wants the other to pay fees.

Another easy source is your past experience. If you practiced with a firm before you started your own practice, then you know what rates your former firm charged. Those also can be a guidepost.

A third source is how busy you are. If you are rushing from file to file and constantly busy, then you should either charge more or hire an associate. If you raise your fees, then your work volume may go down, but your income will go up. Also you will be able to spend time with your family and friends without your pen in one hand and your smartphone in the other. If you hire and train an associate, then you will have the financial reward of leveraging your talent and energy and the professional reward of passing along to another some of the skills that you've learned.

You can get some fee information from your own clients. Many will have hired other lawyers for other tasks and will tell you what their other attorneys have charged.

If you do bill by the hour, record your time every day. From an informal survey and some expensive personal experience, I've concluded that billable time decays at a rate of about 20 percent a day. If you work 8 hours for clients on Monday and don't record your time until Tuesday, you'll remember only about 6.4 hours of your Monday time. If you wait until Wednesday, you'll recall about 5 hours, and if you wait until Thursday, you'll record only about 4 hours. Develop the habit of recording your time every day. You can record your time by typing it directly into your timekeeping and billing software or by writing it on a full-size time log that you or your assistant will transcribe to your billing system later on (no sticky notes, please), or by recording it in your calendar as you make and receive phone calls and pick up files on which to work.

2. Flat Fees, With and Without Milestones

I'd like to suggest that you propose flat fees for projects you can easily define. For example, you may be able to set a flat fee for advising the purchaser of a house. You may be able to set a flat fee for providing a legal opinion in a commercial financing. Flat fees work best where there is little variation in how much time projects of that type will take, and where the client is looking mainly for the result rather than for unusual expertise. The more predictable the project, the more you should consider flat fees. For instance, if in your experience advising a homebuyer takes five to six hours, including reviewing the title report, negotiating the agreement, reading the loan documents, and answering whatever other questions the client may have, you can set a fixed fee based on that average. People who don't want to pay you $400 per hour for five hours of work may be perfectly content to pay $2,000 for the project. Your clients do not care how many hours of work it will take you to complete their project, but they are interested and usually concerned with how much you will charge for the entire project—what your total fee will be. You can charge a fixed fee of $X for which you will read and edit the sale agreement, review the title report and explain it to your client, read the loan documents and confirm to your client that the terms match the offered loan, and read and comment on the closing documents.

It has long puzzled me how a contractor can propose a fixed fee for a project that will take 40 people six months, and a lawyer cannot set a fixed fee for a project that will take one person 10 days. You may not know exactly how long a project will take you, but you are in a better position to come closer than anybody else can. Your clients come to you because they want you to remove some uncertainty in their life. Being able to quote and set a fixed fee is an easy way to remove the client's first uncertainty at the very start of your engagement.

Many projects are amenable to fixed fees. An investor client who is refinancing a large project will look to you for two major tasks: reading and negotiating the loan documents and giving the lender an opinion of borrower's counsel. These two tasks overlap: to give your opinion you will necessarily have to read the loan documents. In negotiating the loan documents, you will be proposing revisions to any terms that violate the laws of your state so that you will be able to give a clean legal opinion that the lender's counsel will accept. Your client will be billed a fixed amount by the lender's counsel and may be more willing to agree to pay you a fixed fee to negotiate the loan documents and give an opinion of borrower's counsel than to pay you by the hour and risk this loan being the refinance that spirals out of control.

If an engagement will last longer than a few months, include milestones for points at which you will earn fees for having completed parts of the project. Let's say that a client engages you to negotiate the purchase of a distressed loan from a bank, to then foreclose on the loan, repossess the property, and obtain a land use approval for the client's business to move into the property. You could charge for your services by the hour, or you could quote a fixed fee for the entire project. The problem with charging a fixed fee for the entire project is that it may take you six months or a year to complete the project. As an alternative to charging a single fee when you've obtained the land use approval (which might, after all, be denied, making your fee unexpectedly contingent), you could also break your fee down into stages, payable as you complete certain milestones along the way: $A for completing the loan purchase, payable when the purchase closes; $B when you complete the foreclosure; $C when you obtain possession of the property; and $D when you obtain the land use approval.

Don't be bashful about quoting and setting a fixed fee for a project. You paid a lot of money in tuition to learn the skills of a lawyer. You spent more than 1,000 hours in school learning your craft. You may have spent thousands more hours honing and improving your skills since then. Prospective clients know that lawyers do not work for free, and they expect to pay a fair amount for a job well done. Your fees may represent a lot of money to your clients, and they are hiring you to get the benefit of your work. If you believe that you are providing value to your clients, then you should not be afraid to tell them what your work is worth, and your clients will appreciate knowing in advance what they will pay and when.

3. Contingent and Success Fees

As lawyers, we think of contingent fees as the province of litigators who represent plaintiffs, particularly in personal injury cases, who will charge a fee that is not tied to any hourly rate but is a portion of the recovery, often tied to the stage of the case. For example, a plaintiff's personal injury lawyer might charge a client 20 percent of the recovery if the case is settled without filing a complaint, 33 percent if it is settled after filing a complaint and more than 30 days before trial, and 40 percent if it is settled within 30 days of the trial date, or if it proceeds to trial and judgment. If there is no recovery, then there is no fee, but the client must still pay the court costs and disbursements.

In the personal injury practice model, a contingency fee works because almost always the only remedy the plaintiff seeks is money as compensation for injuries, and it's easy to divide a sum of money between lawyer and client. Business-side real estate practice doesn't fit well with the contingency model because often the result the client wants isn't money and isn't divisible. A contingent fee for projects that, unlike trying a case, require the agreement of the other side also could put the client's interests at odds with your financial interest. For instance, it would be odd to charge a contingency fee to draft a lease, payable only if the other party signs the lease, and it would also set up a conflict of interest between the lawyer and the client. The lawyer can best protect the client's interests by including provisions in the lease to protect the client against the errors of the other party (e.g., by including a provision to allow a landlord client to change the locks if the tenant is five days late in paying rent). However, the lawyer is more likely to earn the contingent fee if the lawyer writes a lease with fewer protections for the landlord. The landlord's lawyer's interest in earning a fee is in direct conflict with the landlord's interest in having a strong and enforceable lease.

A contingency fee works better if the project is more adversarial, and it doesn't have to be a percentage of the recovery. You can charge a contingent fee in a matter that doesn't have a money recovery (e.g., charging a fixed fee of $X to handle a nonjudicial foreclosure through the foreclosure sale, payable only if and when the foreclosure is complete). The fixed but contingent fee that you quote should be larger than the fixed noncontingent fee that you would charge for the same foreclosure because you're taking on the risk that the borrower will file bankruptcy, sue to enjoin the foreclosure, or take some other action that would make the foreclosure drag on or become impossible to complete.

I have used full contingent fees in one specific area of real estate practice, which is appealing property tax assessments. I have handled more than 200 property tax appeals for a contingent fee of one-half of one year's tax savings. If I accept a contingent property tax engagement and I reduce the client's tax bill by $2,000/year, then I will charge a fee of $1,000. If I don't obtain a tax reduction, then the client does not owe me a fee. I can make this fee model work for property tax appeals because in my state there is no filing fee to appeal a property tax assessment to the county, the time to prepare and present an appeal is limited, and the counties in which I work will group my appeals together so that I can present several in the same session. I can make one trip to the assessor's office or the property tax appeals board serve four or five clients. Once I presented ten appeals in the same morning, one right after another.

Clients like this model because it costs them nothing to have me handle the appeal unless I win. If I win, the county will refund the excess property tax for the year, so the client sees the result of my work in cash in the mailbox. It's a lot less painful for a client to pay a lawyer $1,000 if a $2,000 refund from the government has just arrived in the client's mailbox.

A fee can be partly hourly and partly contingent, or partly fixed and partly contingent. The contingent portion is sometimes called a success fee. I have used success fees from time to time in another sort of real estate dispute in which the client will see the results of my work in cash: eminent domain cases, for which I sometimes charge a fee with both hourly and success components. My fee agreement with a condemnation client might be that I will charge 90 percent of my usual hourly rate, plus a success fee of 15 percent of the amount by which the eventual payment from the government exceeds the best offer that the government made before the client hired me. The percentage by which I would reduce my rates and the success fee that I would charge depend on the amount at stake and on my evaluation of how far the government offer is from my opinion of the value. My fee proposal would be one thing for a client who has been offered $300,000 for property that I think I can show to be worth $350,000, and another thing for a client who has been offered $1,500,000 for property that I think I can show to be worth $2,500,000. In either case, however, I charge the success fee only on the portion of the award that exceeds the government's best offer before I'm hired because the client didn't use my services to obtain that offer.

Rule 1.5 of the Rules of Professional Conduct (RPC) defines a contingent fee as a fee that is "contingent on the outcome of the matter for which the service is rendered." RPC 1.5 allows you to charge a contingent fee except when prohibited by law and in two specific cases, neither of which comes up much in real estate law. RPC 1.5 prohibits a lawyer from charging a fee in a domestic relations matter that is "contingent upon the securing of a divorce or upon the amount of alimony or support, or property settlement in lieu thereof," and also prohibits lawyers from charging a contingent fee for representing a defendant in a criminal case.

B. Asking for Advance Deposits (Retainers) and Managing Client Trust Accounts

The word "retainer" used to mean a fixed amount that a client paid a lawyer every month or every quarter to assure the client that the lawyer would be available to represent the client if necessary. Sometimes the lawyer agreed to do a certain amount of work at no separate charge—the retainer was the fee. Today many lawyers use the word "retainer" more broadly to mean a deposit that the client pays the lawyer before the lawyer starts work, which the lawyer can draw on for fees and costs.

Should you require a new client to pay you a deposit before you take on your first project for the client? Some lawyers require a deposit from the client so that they can be assured that the client is willing to pay for their services. Others make that decision project by project.

My policy is somewhere in between. I don't require deposits for new projects from current or recent clients. If a client comes to me "cold" (not referred by or related to another client, and not someone I've known for some years already) then I will often ask for a deposit that is either 25 percent to 50 percent of my estimated fee for a small project, or about equal to one month's fees and costs for a longer project. If I'm going to have to pay more than nominal fees and costs to third parties (e.g., professional fees to surveyors, substantial filing and recording fees, or fees for experts), I will always ask for a deposit from a new client to cover those costs.

If you do receive a deposit for fees you have not earned yet, handle the deposit in accordance with the regulations of your state bar for unearned fees. The ABA's Model Rules of Professional Conduct (RPCs), adopted in some form as of this writing (2014) by 49 states, the District of Columbia, and the United States Virgin Islands, includes this provision as RPC 1.15(c):

> (c) A lawyer shall deposit into a client trust account legal fees and expenses that have been paid in advance, to be withdrawn by the lawyer only as fees are earned or expenses incurred.

Until you have done the work or incurred the expenses, the deposit is not yours; it is the client's. You must maintain it in a separate trust account, identified as a client trust account. (Some jurisdictions require you to call it a "lawyer trust account," which is the same thing.) You can write checks on the client trust account to pay third parties for expenses incurred for the client, such as recording fees, up to the amount of that client's deposit. You can write checks on the client trust account to pay your fees after you have done the work for which you're withdrawing the fee. I suggest that when you pay your fees from the trust account, you do so by writing a check from the trust account to your operating account, not from the trust account to your personal account or your landlord or anyone else. Because your trust account is subject to inspection and audit by your state regulator, you must keep records of the trust account as clean and straightforward as possible.

Have your trust account checks printed to be unmistakably different from your operating account checks. If your operating account checks are blue, print your trust account checks in yellow or pink, using a different typeface and style, so that you will never mistakenly draw a check on your trust account for an expense that you'd intended to pay from your operating account.

C. Billing Your Fees

If you are charging an hourly fee on a project, then, unless it is a short project or you have a special agreement with your client, you should be sending the client an invoice at a regular time, once a month. The invoice will describe the work you performed, when you did it, and how much you are charging. As bills with due dates tend to be paid faster than bills without due dates, include on your invoices the date of the invoice (your billing software will put dates on your invoices) and include a sentence that states when payment is due. This sentence should match your engagement letter. For instance, if you wrote in your engagement letter that your invoices are due on receipt, then print on your invoices the phrase "due on receipt." If your engagement letter says that your invoices are due 30 days after billing, include on your invoices the phrase "due 30 days from the date of this invoice."

In the 1960s, only the large firms had data processing equipment and software to generate invoices to clients. A typical billing system for a smaller firm of that era used paper records. The lawyers wrote their time entries on carbonless timeslips that were then torn off and placed in the client file. When the file had a lot of timeslips in it, or when the matter was completed, the responsible lawyer would open the file, dictate the time entries into the form of a letter, and send the letter as an invoice to the client. Sometimes the lawyer would read the timeslips and send a letter that said simply "For services rendered in the Acme matter: 24 hours at $30/hour—please remit $720." Early in my father's practice, he and his partner would pay little attention to billing clients until their secretary warned them that the bank balance was getting low. They would then meet at the office on a Saturday, go through the files to see who hadn't been billed for a while, and dictate invoices to be typed and mailed on Monday. Within a few weeks money would come in to replenish the bank balance.

The business of law has progressed since 1962. Billing methods have become more efficient. If you are charging your clients by the hour, then you should be sending bills each month. Clients are used to receiving monthly bills from their other providers, and you need to charge for and be paid for your time to cover your overhead and make a living.

If you are operating as a solo without any staff, then set aside the first or second day of each month to prepare and send your bills for the previous month. Block that time out on your calendar as an appointment with yourself (see Sections XIII.B and XIII.C for more on calendaring) so that you protect the time you need to prepare and send bills against incursions.

If you are operating with staff and not typing your own bills, then your billing cycle will have several parts:

- Finish entering all time and expenses for the prior month.
- Staff will print prebills (draft bills) for you to review.
- You will review all prebills for fairness, accuracy, and timeliness and edit them as necessary.
- Staff will revise the prebills and print and mail the final bills for the month.

Establish a regular schedule for accomplishing these four tasks. When I opened my practice, my office manager and I set up a fixed schedule approximately as follows:

- All time and expenses for the prior month will be entered by noon of the first business day of the current month.
- Prebills will be printed and distributed on the afternoon of the first business day of the month.
- Lawyers' edits of prebills are due back on the second business day of the month.
- At least 95 percent of the bills will be printed, copied, and in the mail on the third business day of the month.

Clients want to be billed promptly, and they will pay more readily for recent service than for old work. Banks and other large businesses have established policies under which they will not pay invoices for work that is more than 90 days in the past, both so they can manage and predict their legal expenses and because they expect their lawyers to be as businesslike as they are themselves.

If you are advising a client on the purchase or sale of a property, you can offer to send your invoice to the escrow company or closing agent, to be paid at closing either from the proceeds of sale if your client is the seller, or as an add-on to your client's deposit, if your client is the buyer. Your client may be willing to pay you at closing if you ask in advance, so that the cost of your services will be on the closing statement with the other expenses where your client's accountant can see it and report it properly on your client's tax return. There is no reason to wait until the first of next month to invoice a client who wants to pay you now.

D. Collecting Your Fees

Most clients want to pay their bills, including the bills that you send for your services. A few simple steps will assist your clients to pay promptly.

First, design your bills to be easy to read, and especially to clearly state what your clients owe. Your billing software will come with several billing templates: several and maybe dozens of different forms for bills. My firm's billing software came with more than 40 templates. But just because your billing software comes with 40+ different bill formats doesn't mean you have to use all 40, any more than you have to use all 40 fonts that come with your word processor. You can handle most of your billing needs with only a few formats:

- A detailed billing format that shows date, description, attorney, hours, and fee, with totals at the end;
- A simple format for small projects that shows the totals only;
- A format that corresponds to your local court requirements for prevailing party fee statements, if you handle real estate litigation regularly;
- A format that corresponds to your local court requirements for fee requests in probate matters, if you expect to handle probates regularly; and

- Special formats for institutional clients that require their invoices to be in a particular form, such as the LEDES forms or client-specific forms.

Regardless of the format, take the time to lay out your basic invoice forms to be clear and attractive. The top of your invoice should show your firm's name, address, and telephone number so that your client can call at once if there is a question about your bill, without having to search for your number. Because your business clients will have to send you a Form 1099-MISC if they pay you $600 or more in one year for your services, print your employer identification number (not your social security number) on your invoices.

Your invoice should also identify the matter by name and number: by name, so that your client can identify it, and by number, so that you can identify it also.

Next, it should describe your work, whether briefly or in detail.

Your invoice should then show the costs and disbursements for which you're charging the client. Identify each disbursement in enough detail so that your client knows what the charge is for. Some software will identify only the vendor unless you add more information. Some clients may be able to figure out that a disbursement of $250 to Acme Court Reporting is for a court reporter at a deposition, but others may not. Make it easy: describe the disbursement as "Acme Court Reporting (Smith deposition) $250." Other vendors may need more description. Your client won't know why you disbursed $50 to Washington County unless you give more information, such as "Washington County—copies of public documents" or "Washington County—recording fee."

The last, or nearly last, bit of information on your bill should be a statement of the total amount due. Clients who do not review each of your time entries in detail will skip to the end to find out how much to send you.

Make it easy for your clients to pay you. Here are three steps you can take to help your clients pay you faster.

First, don't make your clients hunt for an envelope. Larger business clients who print their checks by computer will have their own envelopes that match their check stock, but people and smaller business clients won't. Help them pay you faster. Include a return envelope, preprinted with your name and address. I prefer preprinted envelopes to window envelopes because using preprinted envelopes eliminates one chance for error, which is the client stuffing the invoice and check into the envelope without your address showing through the window. Send your invoices in no. 10 envelopes, which are 9.5 inches wide, and include a preprinted no. 9 return envelope, which is 8.875 inches wide and will fit nicely inside the no. 10 envelope. Don't try to stuff a no. 10 return envelope into another no. 10 envelope. One or both of the envelopes will crinkle or tear, and the effect will look unprofessional.

Second, put stamps on the return envelopes, or buy them with preprinted postage, so that your clients won't have to look for stamps. If you send out 20 invoices a month, then the 20 extra stamps will cost you only about $120/year. It's an inexpensive way to save your clients a small and irksome task. I picked up this point when I received a small package from a client. I opened it to find that she had sent me a robin's egg blue Tiffany & Co. box, sized to hold a ring. Inside the box was not a ring but a roll of stamps and her note to me explaining that she paid most of her bills online without using stamps, and would pay mine faster if I would send her prestamped return envelopes.

For the rest of the engagement I prestamped her return envelopes, and she paid very promptly.

Third, arrange to accept credit cards in payment of your fees.[1] You will pay the bank or credit card processor a charge of about 1.5 percent to 3 percent. You will have the added expense of the credit card fees, but you will collect your fees much faster. Clients who are slow to write checks will happily charge your fees to their credit card, partly for convenience but mostly, I suspect, to earn airline miles.

---

1. The ethical rules of some states can make it difficult to accept credit card payments as advances for fees that you haven't earned yet.

E. Collecting Your Past Due Fees

Even though you send your bills out promptly, some of your clients will not pay promptly. Your engagement letter will have stated how long your client has after receiving the invoice to pay the bill.

If you work in a larger office, then the managers will have some policy for handling clients who do not pay their bills and become delinquent. If you are running your own office, or if your office has no policy on collecting delinquent bills, then you should adopt a policy. A good policy will state when you will call a delinquent client, when you will write, and when you will stop work until brought current. Your policy might be that you will call a delinquent client when an invoice is two weeks past due, write when it is one month past due, write a second letter when it is two months past due, and stop work (if permitted by your engagement letter and the ethics rules) when it is three months past due.

The first reminder letter should be short and polite. Some clients simply misplace bills. Others pay their bills at a fixed time of the month. Still others may have planned to pay you from funds they were expecting to receive from third parties. An absent-minded client may need only the gentlest of reminders to send you a check. Your first letter should be a gentle reminder and not a demand for payment. It can be short and polite.

July 25, 2015

Dear Ms. Client:

I haven't received your payment for our invoice of June 12 in the amount of $1,650, which is now a few weeks past due. Will you please send payment now? Let me know if you've misplaced the invoice and would like another copy. And if you have sent your payment already, please disregard this letter. As always, thank you for engaging us to advise you.

Very truly yours,

SAMPLE LAW FIRM LLP

Robert J. Sample

A follow-up letter can be more direct:

August 25, 2015

Dear Ms. Client:

   I haven't received your payment for our invoice of June 12 in the amount of $1,650, which is now two months past due. I sent you a courtesy notice on July 25 and didn't hear back from you. Will you please send payment immediately? As a reminder, our agreement allows me to stop work if your account is more than XX days past due. If for some reason you can't pay in full now, please call me so that you and I can agree on a payment plan.

Very truly yours,

SAMPLE LAW FIRM LLP

Robert J. Sample

When you represent a client who is trying to collect a consumer debt (e.g., back rent on an apartment), you are subject to federal and state debt collection practices acts. The federal Fair Debt Collection Practices Act (FDCPA, 15 U.S.C. § 1692 and following) applies to your efforts in collecting consumer debts on behalf of your clients. The FDCPA does not cover your efforts to collect nonconsumer debts, and it does not cover your efforts to collect your own debts if you are collecting them in your own name. State law, however, may apply to your efforts to collect your fees from consumers even though you're collecting your own debts and not debts owed to your clients.[2]

---

2. For example, Oregon's debt collection practices act (ORS 646.639 and following) defines "debt collector" without excluding commercial creditors who are collecting their own consumer debts, California's debt collection practices act (Cal. Civ. Code § 1788 and following) covers attorneys who collect debts, whether for themselves or for others, and New York's debt collection practices act (N.Y. G.B.S. Law §601 and following) covers creditors who are collecting consumer claims owed to them.

F. Keeping and Filing Your Bills

If you send out only a few bills each month, you or your assistant can easily sort and file your copies in the appropriate matter files. When you practice grows to the point that you are sending out dozens of invoices each month, it will become more tedious to sort the invoices and file each in its matter file. Instead of filing your copy of each bill in the matter file every month, sort them by name or client number and then keep your copies in a month file: all of your October bills go in one file, your November bills in the next, and so on. After you send an invoice to your client, you will rarely need to read it again. You will be able to answer most of your clients' billing questions by calling up the invoice or the fee or cost entry through your timekeeping and billing program. Only in a few situations have I needed to refer to old invoices. One is when a client has lost my invoice and needs another copy. (Even in that situation, my billing software can print a duplicate invoice.) Another is when a client has sent in a payment that doesn't match an invoice and that doesn't include the invoice number or return sheet. These situations are rare. Save your assistant the time and trouble of filing every invoice and keep them grouped by month until you need to look.

Chapter XII

Managing and Monitoring Your Finances

A. Monitor Your Business Finances

Recording your time and fees promptly and sending invoices to your clients each month are two important steps toward managing and monitoring your business finances. There are several others. Managing the finances of your business includes daily, weekly, monthly, and annual routines, along these lines.

Daily tasks
- Record billable time and fees.
- Record and deposit receipts.

Weekly tasks
- Pay invoices from vendors, charging to client files when appropriate.

Semimonthly tasks
- Pay staff.
- Pay payroll taxes (unless payroll is low enough to qualify for monthly payment).

Monthly tasks
- Pay rent.

135

- Review prebills.
- Print and send invoices to clients.
- Review the list of accounts receivable.
- Prepare a month-end income statement and balance sheet.
- Compare hours to budget.
- Pay payroll taxes (unless payroll is high enough to require semimonthly deposits).
- Review the bank statements and balance the operating account and the trust account.

Quarterly tasks
- Compare income statement to budget.
- Adjust the current budget as necessary.
- Pay your personal estimated income taxes.
- Deposit federal unemployment tax payments.

Annual tasks
- File business income, employment, and unemployment tax returns.
- File your personal income tax return.
- Compare actual performance to budget.
- Prepare budget for the upcoming year.

As part of organizing your office, assign these tasks among you and your staff, with target days of the month on which each will be accomplished.

1. Watch Your Accounts Receivable Closely

One of the most important accounts to monitor is accounts receivable (A/R), the money that your clients owe you for your work. A good accounts receivable report will tell you not only how much your clients owe you but also how long the debts have been running and when you last received a payment. You may not worry too much about a client for whom you're doing only a little bit of work each month and who owes you a few thousand dollars, but if you see from the report that the client hasn't paid you anything for six months, you will want to find out why. You should also be reluctant to take on a new matter for that client if he or she isn't paying you for the current matters.

When should you worry about the total of your accounts receivable? Two common ways to measure accounts receivable are by their average age, and by the number of days or months of billings that the accounts equal. Suppose that you bill $30,000 each month and you have taken to heart my advice to send your bills promptly. Suppose also that you expect many of your clients to pay within 30 days and all of them to pay within 60 days. Immediately before billing day (let's say it's March 5) what should your accounts receivable total? You should have received some portion, let's say half, of the bills that you sent in February for January time, and you should have received almost all of the bills that you sent in January for December time. So your A/R should include maybe $10,000 of the February bills and maybe $2,000 of the January bills, plus any aged A/R that is on your books from clients that you've terminated for nonpayment or who have gone broke. You should have virtually no A/R from the bills that you sent in December or earlier.

You would then expect your accounts receivable to be about $42,000 immediately after you print and send your March bills for February time. The $42,000 is 1.4 times your average monthly billings, so you can say that you have 1.4 months of accounts receivable. (Many firms would envy you for having clients who pay so promptly.) If you have $60,000 of accounts receivable, then you have 2.0 months' worth of receivables, which is not as desirable and is cause for some concern. And if you have $120,000 of accounts receivable, then you have 4.0 months of receivables, which should be a serious warning sign that something is wrong.

A second way to evaluate your receivables is by their aging. How old are they? Credit managers age receivables by days: 30 or less, 31 to 60, 61 to 90, 91 to 120, and older than 120 days. Your billing software can generate an aging report for you. You should read it every month and make phone calls or send reminder letters to the slow payers, particularly if you're continuing to do their work.

If your bills are fair and timely and your clients are solvent and willing to pay, then you should have almost no receivables that are older than 90 days. One of the many positive things about representing long-term real estate investors is that they pay their bills punctually. I have only about three days' worth of receivables that are older than 90 days.

2. Pay Your Payroll Taxes When Due

When cash runs low, small businesses are sometimes tempted to delay depositing payroll taxes with the government. The owners believe that it's more important to pay their other bills so that their suppliers will not cut them off, or that when the late-paying client finally pays, the business can send in the taxes, paying whatever the penalties might be. The Internal Revenue Service (IRS), the owners think, will be slow to notice that the tax deposits haven't arrived.

This is a dangerous practice. (I would print this sentence in red ink if I could.)

Taxes that you withhold from your employees' paychecks are not your money. Under Section 6672 of the Internal Revenue Code, you hold those funds in trust for the government. If you underwithhold or underdeposit the payroll taxes by accident and you are discovered, you may escape with only a penalty. If, however, the IRS believes that you underwithheld or underdeposited on purpose, then you are subject to criminal prosecution. If you are convicted of tax fraud, your state bar may find you to be unfit to practice law.

The IRS is not your bank.[1] Don't borrow its money. Pay your employees through a payroll service such as ADP or Paychex so that the payroll taxes will be calculated and deposited correctly and on time based on the payroll report you submit.

3. Watch Out for Scams

People who masquerade as suppliers and vendors will try to scam you out of money by sending you invoices for things you haven't bought or by sending solicitations in the form of an invoice. The nature and variety of scams change so frequently—they morph like bacteria—that the advice I can give you can be only general. Within that variety, however, scams can be sorted into several broad categories.

First is the imitation invoice. Until publication of telephone books fell off, I received one or two mailings a month that looked rather like invoices,

---

1. Another reason not to mess with the IRS on your payroll taxes is that its parent organization operates a prison system.

offering listings in the Yellow Pages. In the United States, "Yellow Pages" is not a registered trademark but is a generic description for telephone directories of businesses, sorted by type, so many companies use it to describe their directories. The statements were for small amounts, always less than $100, and an inattentive clerk who knew that the firm was listed in the Yellow Pages might easily pay one as a matter of routine. In an unobtrusive location, the statements would bear a disclaimer, such as "This is not an invoice," easy for the casual eye to miss.

Second is the office products telephone survey. A caller asks for the brand name and model number of the office copier as part of a survey, getting as an apparent afterthought the name of the receptionist or office manager who answered (let's call her "Donna"). A few weeks later a shipment of toner cartridges will arrive, likely to be unpacked and stored as a matter of routine. The toner cartridges fit the copier, after all. Then a week later an invoice will arrive charging an inflated price, stating that "Donna" ordered the toner cartridges.

More technically up-to-date is the Internet directory listing. I get these once or twice a month by e-mail. The notice requests me to confirm my company's listing in the such-and-such directory, usually described as a book to be printed and distributed to large corporations and to make any corrections on the attached form. The form has a space for me to sign to approve the listing and corrections. Hidden in the fine print is a promise to pay hundreds of dollars for the listing in the directory.

A scam that your business and investor clients will see more often than you will is the mailing made up to look like an official state mailing that tells them that state law requires their corporation to prepare annual minutes and file an annual report, and then offers to do the work for a fixed sum. The perpetrators design these forms to look something like official forms and hope that the recipients will pay the unnecessary fees.

Be alert for these and other attempts to cozen you out of your money. If you do sign one of these forms by mistake, as a lawyer you'll have a hard time persuading a court that you should be excused from paying what you've promised because you didn't read the contract.

B. Keep Your Clients' Money Rigorously Separate from Your Own

Even though you do not hold a license as a trust company, whenever you receive funds from your clients that you have not earned or that are not intended to pay your fees, you have become a trustee, and you have undertaken a fiduciary responsibility to the owner of the funds. It may happen that you represent the seller of some real estate, and the buyer, represented neither by a lawyer nor by a broker, brings you a check for the earnest money, payable to your office.

Those funds are not yours; they belong to your client until you apply them in accordance with your client's instructions. Do not commingle the funds of your client with your own funds.

This would seem a simple principle to follow, and yet it ensnares lawyers across the county every year, particularly personal injury lawyers (who may receive large settlements on behalf of their clients), probate lawyers (who may be executors of their clients' estates, with control over the funds), and real estate lawyers (who may receive earnest money and act as closing agents).

Commingling funds is an easy way to attract unwanted attention from the bar association because the lawyer's intent is not relevant. A longtime real estate investor in another state tells me, "Every real estate attorney in this area who has been disbarred has suffered that fate for commingling funds. Some were extremely sloppy with their escrow accounts, while others were tempted into fraud or outright theft."

Protect your reputation and your license. Keep meticulous records of your clients' funds. Do not draw trust account checks on uncleared or uncertain funds. Do not borrow from your trust account. And do not delegate signature authority on your trust account to your staff. You are responsible to your clients and to the state bar for every dollar entrusted to you.

Chapter XIII

Managing Your Time and Workload

A. Managing Your Time

1. Know the Claimants on Your Time

Abraham Lincoln said that a lawyer's time is his stock in trade. Your time is your inventory. For your practice to succeed, you have to allocate it wisely among those who are competing for it.

The claimants on your time are more numerous than the traditional four categories of work, home, play, and rest. The work claimants alone include at least these categories:

- Meeting with clients;
- Reading and writing letters and agreements;
- Managing your office;
- Editing your prebills;
- Attending continuing legal education classes;
- Reading and answering e-mail;
- Serving on boards of nonprofit organizations;
- Meeting with prospective clients;
- Responding to callers looking for free advice;
- Responding to callers who want to sell you something;
- Lunch because you're hungry;
- Lunch to network, market, or talk with clients;
- Attending bar association meetings;
- Evaluating prospective vendors, and;

• Interviewing prospective employees.

How you allocate your time among all of these things depends on your specific practice and on the degree to which your schedule is controlled by others. If you mainly represent landlords and tenants in evictions, the court's schedule becomes your schedule. You may have to reserve 8:30 to noon every day to be available to be in court, even if on some days you have no court appearances.

You have more control over your schedule if you have an office practice. You can decide on which days and at what times to see clients, meet with your staff, and work on projects. Even the best scheduling can be undone if you let interruptions disrupt your plans, and for most of us that means taking back control of your time from your telephone and your e-mail.

2. Control Interruptions: The Office Telephone

For eight years before I became a lawyer, I worked at a desk in a 30-employee real estate business that the owner managed. Although the owner never made a point of it, every new employee quickly noticed one of the owner's business practices. He was on the telephone a lot, but he would not answer the telephone while he was meeting with any of the staff, not even to take a message. He placed a higher priority on the person he was with than on an unknown caller. If a staffer came by to talk with him while he was placing a call, he would stop dialing, hang up the phone, and talk with the staffer.

Too many people, lawyers included, reverse this priority. To them, the unknown person calling is more important than the client or coworker sitting in the office. At least, that's the impression they give to their client when they interrupt their discussion with the client to answer a call.

The telephone is a great communication instrument, but it is also a great interrupter. We're trained from childhood to answer the phone promptly and not to let it ring. What was a good habit in childhood is a mixed blessing in the workplace, for the practical reason that if you are working on a project at your desk and you break off your work to answer the telephone about some other matter, you lose two portions of your time. First, it will take you a few moments to pull back into your mind the subject of the telephone call and perhaps to summon the file, so you will be less efficient and less effective on the phone call. Second, when the call is over it will take you rather longer to get back up to speed on the project that you set aside to take the phone call.

When a client is in your office, the most important button on your telephone is the do not disturb (DND) button, the one that shows the client who is paying for that hour that he or she is receiving all of that hour, without interruption. The only two exceptions are if you are truly waiting for an unavoidable call (e.g., a call from the court clerk that the jury has returned) or if you're waiting for a call about that client's matter. Unless the President is one of your clients (which means that you don't need this book), even a call from the White House can wait until your client meeting is over.

Some projects can be done in small pieces. Others require or deserve more attention. If you are writing a short demand letter or cover letters to your clients or if you are editing your prebills, you can set the task aside to answer the telephone without losing much of your mental work on the project at hand. But if you are working out a bit of difficult legal reasoning or trying to harmonize two cases, or reading and editing a long lease, when you interrupt your thinking, you will lose some of the thread of what you were doing, and you will have to do it over again to regain your place.

I recommend three strategies for mastering your telephone.

First, use the DND button liberally to protect your best thinking time from the ringtone.

Second, update your voice mail announcement every day so that callers know that you are in the office and when you will be available to talk or able to return calls. I record a new message every business day. A caller who hears yesterday's message today will know that I haven't been to the office yet.

My daily voice mail message follows this form: "This is Dean Alterman. It's Tuesday, I'm in the office most of the day today, and in client meetings from 9 to 11 and from 2 to 3. At the tone please leave your name, your telephone number, and a message of reasonable length. I will return your call as soon as I can." The meeting times I list include my self-appointments: my private thinking and working time. In a few words, I've told callers that I've come into the office today and when I will be available. A caller who hears my message at 9:15 will know that I won't be able to return the call until sometime after 11:00.

If I am preparing for a hearing or have some other major commitment, I will record a message like this one: "This is Dean Alterman. It's Wednesday. I'm in the office today, but after 11:00 I will be preparing for a hearing and will not be available to talk until after the hearing tomorrow. If you are calling after 11:00 on Wednesday, I will return your call on Thursday after the hearing. If this is an emergency, please send me an e-mail as I will be reading e-mails this afternoon." My message on the day of the hearing might be: "This is Dean Alterman. It's Thursday. I will be in a hearing out of the office most of the day protecting private property rights.[1] At the tone please leave your name, your telephone number, and a message of reasonable length. I will return your call this evening or Friday morning."

Third, have an easy system to organize your phone messages. I use a Priority Management product called the Voicemail/Phone Lot, now unfortunately discontinued, which is an 8 ½ x 11–inch printed pad with 40 lines to the page, printed on both sides, so each sheet will record 80 calls. Each line is intended to note one call. The pad is organized into columns: date, time, name/message, phone number, and follow-up. I don't use my message pad to take detailed notes about my return call or to transcribe the entire message, but simply to write enough of the message for me to know what it's about and who to call back. My notes on one line of the pad for a voice mail might read like this:

Date	Time	Name/Message	Phone	Follow-up
8/24	10:15 a	*Addison Cutlip re Braxton Gardens title report*	*(302) 555-1212*	

In the follow-up column I will note whether I called back or sent an e-mail, what time I called or e-mailed, and whether I spoke with the caller or left a voice mail. If I want to save the entire voice mail, then I will type it, or have it typed, and save it to the client file.

---

1. I will use my voice mail message to describe in general terms what I'm working on only if it fairly describes the issue that I'm advocating for my clients that day and if I am not breaching a client confidence or violate an ethical rule.

I also make similar notes about many of the client calls that I place and receive so that at the end of the day I have a record of the people I spoke with or left messages for. Occasionally these notes are useful, as for instance if a caller says, "I called you five times and you never answered," I can consult my notes and reply, "You left me a message on August 5 at 2:42. I called you back at 4:45 and didn't hear back from you since then." Some callers will be irritated that they called you five times without a reply but will have forgotten that you did return the first call and they didn't leave their name or number for the second, third, fourth, and fifth calls.

3. Controlling Interruptions: Your Cell Phone

If you are often in your car and only rarely at the office, then your cell phone is an essential tool for keeping in touch with your clients and transacting business. If you are usually in the office during the workday, then clients will rarely call you on your cell phone during office hours because they will call your office phone first and leave messages on your voice mail. Your cell phone at the office is just another distraction, something to beep at you while you're thinking through a complex problem or meeting with a client.

Imagine this situation for a moment. You are in your office conferring with a client about an upcoming hearing, and your cell phone rings. You have four choices:

- Take the call;
- Look to see who is calling, and then take the call;
- Look to see who is calling, and decide not to take the call; or
- Don't look and don't take the call.

Which would you do? Pick your answer before you read on.

Did you pick one of the first three choices? Consider the message that the first three choices send to the client who is sitting in your office.

- Taking the call says that your client is less important than the person who is calling because you would rather talk to an unknown caller than to the client who is sitting on the other side of your desk.

- Looking at the caller ID and then taking the call also says that your client might be less important than the caller, and now that you know who the caller is, you are certain that your client is less important than the person who is calling.
- Looking at the caller ID but not taking the call says that some callers are more important than your client, but this particular caller isn't.

Only the fourth choice shows your client that he or she is getting your undivided attention and that, for the duration of your meeting, the client is the most important person in your world.

If you agree with me that the fourth choice is the only proper choice and that you should never answer your cell phone while you are meeting with your client, then it follows that you don't need your phone to ring because you aren't going to take the call even if it does ring. Therefore, turn your cell phone off, or at least mute the ringtone, when you are meeting with clients.

If your cell phone will ring when clients are around to hear it, choose a businesslike ringtone or a very soft chime that matches the image that you want your office to convey.[2]

I have two cell phones. One is a smartphone that sends and receives e-mail and connects to the Internet. The other is a not-so-smartphone that simply makes and receives phone calls. When I am in my office, I set both to be silent or simply turn them off. I can always check my phones for messages before lunch and at the end of the day. I've set both to use plain and simple ringtones at low volume.

4. Controlling Interruptions: E-Mail

Sixty years ago when people sent business messages by letter through the post office, they expected a prompt response, but "a prompt response" meant a telephone call in a day or two or a reply letter in a week. As we've progressed through the era of the fax machine to that of e-mail, we've redefined what a prompt response means.

E-mails usually arrive within a few seconds after they are sent. Each arriving e-mail is the modern version of the ringing phone, demanding to

---

2. Rimsky-Korsakov did not write "Flight of the Bumblebee" to be played on a cell phone.

be answered. And like the ringing phone, each arriving e-mail interrupts your train of thought.

E-mail programs can be set to ping when a message arrives. Unless you receive only two or three e-mails a day, turn the pinging off. If every workday you receive 50 e-mails (not a high number for an active lawyer), then a ping will interrupt you every 10 minutes. If you and two nearby coworkers receive 50 e-mails at work each day, then the hollow pings from your computer and theirs will distract you from your work every three minutes, and your suite will sound like the sonar station in a submarine.

If you answer each e-mail when it comes in, the messages will turn your workday into Swiss cheese: full of holes that add volume but not substance. I answer e-mails in four bursts a day. In the morning immediately after I plan my work for the day, I will take 15 minutes or so to read and answer or forward new e-mail. Shortly before lunch I will do the same for the morning's e-mail. When I return from lunch I will read and answer the e-mails that came in while I was out. Before I go home for the night I will read the afternoon's e-mails.

At other times of the day when I'm in between projects, I will look at the senders and subject lines of my unread messages, and if one is important or relates to what I'm doing that day, I will read it. My overall goal, which I strongly recommend to you, is to assign specific blocks of time to dealing with your e-mail and to protect other blocks of time from e-mail distractions so that you can use those blocks to work on longer projects.

One exception to my rule is that if I am in an e-mail conversation with a client, I will continue that conversation while the client is responding quickly or if it relates to what I'm working on at that moment. Here are two examples. My client and I may be on a conference call with several other people, and we may text or e-mail between ourselves during the call so that we can communicate without being overheard. I may be working on a lease for a client and have some questions about the business points. If I send my questions and get a response promptly, that leaves a few points unanswered, I will respond promptly. In that case the messages aren't interrupting my current project because I am sending and reading them to get information that I need for the current project.

If you link your smartphone to your office e-mail, then when you are not in the office you can use your smartphone to answer messages that require only a short response and that don't need attachments from your office files. I use my smartphone to read and answer e-mail when I'm away from my desk and not with a client so that I can reduce the stack of unread e-mails that await my return.

B. Managing Your Workload

We think of docketing systems mainly as a way to track deadlines, and more so for litigation than for business and real estate transactions. A good system to track deadlines is essential. Without a good system, a lawyer will miss deadlines, make clients unhappy, and risk malpractice claims. But tracking deadlines is only one time management function; planning your work is the other.

Consider an example from litigation practice. You represent the defendant in a dispute over title to a tract of land. On June 1, the plaintiff filed a motion for summary judgment. Your state's rules give you 21 days to respond to the motion, so your response is due on June 22. When the motion was filed and served, you promptly wrote the due date of June 22 on your calendar and entered it into your office's docketing system.

Both of those steps are good. I suggest that you do a third step, which is to reserve the time it will take to research and write the response. If you expect to take ten hours to research and write your response to the motion, then block out the ten hours now on your calendar, whether paper or electronic, just as you would block out time for a court appearance or client appointment. You know that you will need the time, so reserve it now. Shop foremen and production managers use a similar method to schedule jobs and allocate time on a factory's principal machines. You are the principal machine of your factory, and you need to protect the time that you need for projects against less important interruptions.

Some interruptions are unavoidable. If you've booked the afternoon of June 8 for three of the hours you will need for the project and another client has an emergency, you can handle the emergency—but you must then choose and reserve another three-hour slot for the portion of the work that you were going to do on June 8.

If you do not reserve time for your longer projects well in advance, then it will be all too easy when the emergency comes up on June 8 to push the time for the response aside because you still have two weeks before your response is due, which sounds like a lot of time in which to do a ten-hour project. And it is a lot of time . . . until on June 20 you realize that your response is due the day after tomorrow and you haven't started it yet because you've let other demands push it off of your calendar.

In a transactional real estate practice, you must track not just the expected closing date of a transaction but also various notification and due diligence dates, such as the buyer's deadline to exercise or waive an inspection contingency or to object to exceptions on the title report or to provide proof of financing. It's become the practice in my area for the commercial brokers involved in a sale to prepare and send a memorandum of critical dates immediately after the buyer and seller have signed the purchase and sale agreement. Enter these dates in three places: your electronic calendar, your paper calendar, and in the file. Because you will refer to the broker's memorandum throughout the transaction, don't put it in the general correspondence folder where it will get buried beneath the flood of printed e-mail messages, "welcome letters" from the escrow company, and other correspondence. Put it with the sale agreement. I discuss this point more in Section VI.H on how to design and implement your filing system.

C. Managing Your Calendar

Some of my friends who rely entirely on their computer's electronic calendars will enter deadlines and appointments as they come up, but will review their schedule only one day at a time, sometimes one week at a time. Today's electronic calendar lists only today's appointments and today's due dates. Microsoft Outlook allows the user to look at a day, a week, a month, or a custom range of dates, but the larger the date range, the less information shows for each day. If you docket advance warnings so that (to continue with my example) on June 8 a message pops up that your response to the motion for summary judgment is due in 2 weeks, then you do get that reminder, but when you click on it, it goes away again and may pass out of mind until June 15 when the one-week reminder pops up. The one-month view of your electronic calendar may not show enough information for you to tell your deadlines apart from your appointments.

I use three calendar systems. One is the calendar function of Microsoft Outlook. In it, I enter my appointments and deadlines with advance warnings. Next is our office's docketing system, in which court deadlines are generated to follow prepackaged rules. Third and most important to me is my paper calendar, which is in a three-ring binder with inserts that I purchase from Priority Management. FranklinCovey makes a similar product, called the Franklin Planner. Generically these are often called planner systems or time management systems. The ancestor of all of these systems is the Day-Timer, designed to fit into a wallet-sized carrier rather than onto a desktop, and much favored by people in sales who move around a lot and prefer a more portable system than a desktop planner. The Day-Timer is also available in an 8½ ×11" size, called "folio."

The binder can open flat and zip shut. It lies open on my desk during the workday so that I can add appointments, notes, deadlines and tasks to it. I zip it shut and take it home at night. Its advantage to me over a solely electronic calendar is that it contains several different scales of calendar. Each month in the current year is spread over two pages with squares for each day in which I can write appointments, deadlines, and reminders. At the end of each week is more space for reminders that aren't tied to a specific day, or for which the box for that day doesn't have enough room. The months section stays in my calendar for the entire year.

A separate section holds one page for each day of the current month. At the beginning of each month I remove and discard the pages for the month just ended, copy the appointments and reminders for the new month from the month pages to the day pages, and insert the new month's day pages into the planner.

A third section holds room to plan further ahead—calendar cards for the next two years, at two pages for each year, which I think of as the plan-ahead cards. In October of each year I buy the month and day cards for the next year, and I insert the month cards for the coming year into my notebook. At the beginning of each year I copy the new year's information from the plan-ahead card for the new year to the month pages for the new year, and I remove and save the month pages for the year just ended. I have used the same system for more than 20 years. The two decades of month pages fit into two three-ring binders and serve as a cryptic diary of my business life since 1990.

I've added one refinement to the calendar system, which is a package of pens in eight different colors to replace the mechanical pencil that came with the system. I keep the pens in the notebook and I use the pens to color-code my calendar. I use red for court dates, public hearings, and deadlines. Client appointments are blue, business travel plans are purple, nonprofit board meetings are in green, dates relating to my son are in orange, and other family and personal appointments are in pink. I use light blue to reserve time to work on specific projects. Black has a special meaning and doesn't mark appointments or future activities. Rather, as the day progresses I use black to note on the page for that day the telephone calls I've made or received, which is useful when I'm entering my time for the day into our billing system. I use the same color codes on the day cards as I do for the month cards and the plan-ahead cards.

My color-coding system means that I can look at the two pages for the current month and see what days have deadlines, what days have hearings, and what days I have family events. I can tell at a glance what days are filled with meetings and conference calls and what days are available for me to work on projects.

Whether you have three calendar systems as I do, or have only two, do not rely on only one system. Think of your second calendar as akin to backing up your hard disk drive. Paper calendars can be lost or destroyed. Electronic systems can crash. However good your electronic system may be, have at least some part of your calendar on paper. And however good your paper system may be, have something on computer. If one system fails you, you will still have the information from the other system.

Time planner products mentioned in Section XIII.C:

- The Day-Timer, produced by ACCO Brands and available through http://www.daytimer.com/daytimerstore.

- The Franklin Planner, produced by FranklinCovey Co. and FC Organizational Products LLC and available through http://franklinplanner .fcorgp.com/store.
- The Priority Manager, produced by Priority Management International Inc. and available through http://www.prioritymanagement.com.

Chapter XIV

Communicating with Your Clients

Bar associations will tell you that one of the most common complaints clients have about their lawyers is that the lawyers don't communicate with the clients. It's easy for us to become so busy doing the work that our clients demand that we forget to tell our clients that we are doing it.

One simple way to communicate with your clients—to my surprise, many lawyers don't take this opportunity to communicate with their clients—is to send your clients a copy of every document that comes into or goes out from your office about their transaction. With some of them you might include a short letter of explanation, for example, "Here is a copy of the preliminary title report on the property you are buying. I have reviewed it. I don't see anything unusual. You should save the title report for your file, but you don't need to do anything in response. Call me if you have any questions." Here's another example: "I'm pleased to enclose the deed for the Marshfield property. It was recorded on June 22. You don't need to do anything with this deed except to file the deed with your other papers on this transaction. It has been a pleasure to work with you on this purchase."

Your client who receives something from you that comes with no explanation will want to know two things: First, what does it mean? Second, must the client do something in response? Your client will look to you to answer those two questions.

Imagine that you are the client. You have sold a piece of real estate and are carrying back a mortgage from the buyer. Your lawyer sends you the recorded mortgage. If you are not an experienced real estate investor, you may not know what to do with the mortgage, and you expect your lawyer to tell you.

Consider the difference between these two cover letters:

Dear Mr. Client:

Enclosed please find the recorded mortgage on Blackacre from Blackacre Acquisition Corp. to Blackacre Investment Co.

Very truly yours,

Curt Lawyer

Dear Mr. Client:

Here is the original mortgage from the buyer, Blackacre Acquisition Corp., to your company Blackacre Investment Co. that secures the repayment of the financing that you provided to the buyer. The mortgage was recorded on December 4, 2014, at Document No. 2014-12345, County Records. You should have received the original promissory note, signed by the buyer, from the title company. You do not have to do anything in response to this letter, but please keep the mortgage in a safe place together with the original promissory note as you will have to produce them when the buyer pays off the note.

It was a pleasure to assist you with this sale.

Very truly yours,

Les Curt Lawyer

Keep in mind that some clients will read your words literally. The sale agreement you drafted or negotiated last week states that the buyer will deposit earnest money and will pay the rest of the purchase price, or at least the down payment, "in cash at closing." A real estate investor told me that when she sold a convenience store property to an unrepresented operator, the buyer paid the down payment "in cash at closing" as contracted: $36,000 in cash in a grocery bag accumulated from receipts at his other store. Once, when my father was representing the seller of a commercial property, the buyer showed up at his office with $90,000 in cash in a briefcase to pay for the property.[1] If your client may not know that the requirement to pay the purchase price "in cash at closing" can be satisfied with a cashier's check or a wire transfer, you should say so. More generally, give your clients clear written instructions on what they must do in a transaction. If they are not sophisticated investors, or if they have never before bought or sold a piece of real estate, they will appreciate having your instructions on hand so that they are not embarrassed at closing by having forgotten something that the other parties might be taking for granted that they would know, even if it is something so basic as having identification on hand to show to the notary. Help your clients to not be surprised.

You should copy your client on every letter you send out about the matter. Things that seem of no consequence to the lawyer may be important to your client. If opposing counsel is being difficult, one way to let your client know is to tell your client that opposing counsel is being difficult. A better way to let your client know is by sending copies of every letter that you and the opposing lawyer exchange. Your client may agree with you and understand that the delays in the transaction are not your fault. On the other hand, your client may decide that what you and the other lawyer are arguing about isn't important to him or her and ask you to stop.

Another way to communicate with your client is to write your client a short note even when nothing has happened. A client who doesn't hear from you for two months doesn't know whether something is happening that you haven't told him or her about, or whether nothing has happened. If you send your client a letter along these lines—"I have heard nothing from the other side since we made our demand last month, let's talk about what you would like me to do next"—then your client will be up to date on the status of the matter and will also know that you are waiting for some further direction from the client.

---

1. This happened in 1965, before the federal government enacted legislation to require financial intermediaries to report cash transactions of $10,000 or more. It was the first time I saw a $500 bill.

Yet another way to communicate with your client is through your statements for your services—through your bills. I strongly recommend the book *How to Draft Bills Clients Rush to Pay* by the late J. Harris Morgan of the Texas Bar.[2] Morgan makes the point that your bill should describe your work, not how a lawyer might describe it, but in terms that the client will understand and appreciate. Err on the side of being overdescriptive. Show your client the value you are bringing to the transaction. For instance, instead of describing your work as "Read title report and exceptions," you can describe it as "Read title report and exceptions; check for encroachments; confirm that none of the exceptions affect the intended use of the property." Now you are showing your client not just what you have done but why you did it.

It's also important to communicate with your clients when you expect the final bill to run above your initial estimate. Clients hate unwelcome surprises, especially expensive ones. When you learn that the fee will be higher than you estimated, you can send your client a letter like this: "When you hired me, I told you that I thought your total fee would be between $6,000 and $10,000. As you know, John Doe has filed for bankruptcy and the property is in foreclosure. I did not include in my estimate an allowance for my time to respond to Mr. Doe filing for bankruptcy nor to appear in bankruptcy court to respond to the foreclosure. I am sorry to have to tell you that for these reasons my total fee will be somewhat higher, in the range of $10,000 to $15,000." Your client will not be happy to get your letter, but your client will be even more unhappy to receive a large and unexpected final bill for twice the amount of your initial estimate.

You should also look for ways to provide extra value to your clients. Here are two examples. If you represent the owner of a multitenant building, from time to time the owner will ask you to draft a lease to a new tenant or to extend the lease of an existing tenant. You are probably opening an individual matter for each tenant so that you can index the tenant in your conflict system and have a file with the leasing information for that tenant. You can add value for your client by making a separate file

---

2. The ABA is now publishing the second edition of this book, with Jay G. Foonberg as coauthor.

for the building that has copies of all the leases, so that if an issue comes up with the building, you can easily locate and read all the existing leases at once without having to call for five or six or ten separate files. Having a separate file that includes all the leases is especially useful if your client has been giving exclusive use protections to some of the tenants. If your client calls wanting a lease for a prospective new tenant, you can quickly lay your hands on the existing leases and verify what exclusive uses your client has already granted.

Another way to add value for the client is to add to the file on the building the promissory note and trust deed for the building's financing. If you represented your client in the financing, you have a large file with drafts of the promissory note, the trust deed, and the other financing documents, none of which you will probably ever need to refer to again. You and your client will, however, need to refer to the final promissory note and trust deed when your client sells or refinances the property. Make an extra copy of the note and trust deed and put them in the same file with the leases. If your client calls with a question about the prepayment penalty, that way you can find the promissory note and answer quickly. You may be able to find the promissory note faster than your client can. Your client will appreciate the fast service.

Another way to add value for your client is to send the client information about the client's tenants (or about the client's landlord) that the client may not know. If your landlord client has rented to a chain store, the client may miss a news story about the tenant closing ten stores in other cities. Your client will appreciate knowing this information. Your client will also remember that you are the one who provided it.

I wrote earlier about the importance of sending clients engagement letters that spell out who the client is and what you are doing for the client. You should also send disengagement letters (also called file-closing letters) when you are finished doing the job you were hired to do. Let the client know that you are happy to have done the work, you think you have completed it, and you are now closing your file. Remind the client of any renewal dates for UCC filings, corporate reports, corporate service fees, and the like. Tell your client that he or she should have the original documents for the transaction and originals or copies of the other documents in the transaction. Explain that as you are now closing your file for the matter, you won't be doing any further work on the matter unless you hear from the client.

My disengagement letter reads something like this:

> Dear Mr. X: I am pleased to enclose the original recorded deed transferring Blackacre to you. This deed was recorded on August 15 at book 1227, page 343, Washington County records. Congratulations! This completes your purchase of Blackacre. You should receive a full set of the closing documents from the title company. Our engagement to assist you with your purchase of Blackacre is now complete, and I will close my file. I have appreciated the chance to be of service to you and would be happy to work with you in the future on other legal needs.

I've included another example of a disengagement letter in Appendix 3.

When you finish a transaction, you have an opportunity to do one more thing to provide value to the client. You can assemble the transaction documents, not just with a binder clip or on a disk, but in a three-ring notebook with your firm name on the outside. It will be a continuing reminder to your client that you assisted him or her with the transaction, that you also have the documents in the transaction, and that you are the right lawyer to call if another matter comes up relating to the property. What better place to advertise your practice, in a quiet and dignified way, than on your client's bookshelf?

Chapter XV

Making Your Work Reusable: The Brighter Side of Boilerplate

As your practice grows, you will find that you are preparing the same type of document over and over again. For example, you may find yourself preparing several trust deeds every month, or several loan agreements, or several purchase and sale agreements. It is inefficient to write each agreement from scratch, and it is unfair to the clients to charge them for your time to write an entire agreement from scratch. This discussion expands on some points I touched on in Chapter VI.

The more that you can make your work reusable, the more efficient your practice will be, and the more effectively you will serve your clients

For example, consider these simple drafting points. Let us suppose that Smith hires you to prepare a purchase and sale agreement with Jones. You could write the entire agreement using Smith's name and Jones's name where appropriate. On the other hand, you could define the word "seller" to mean John Smith and the word "buyer" to mean Wilma Jones. In that case, you could reuse the same contract for a similar transaction simply by changing the definitions of "seller" and "buyer" without searching the entire contract for the places where the names of Smith and Jones appear.

Similarly, you could define "Property" to be "the real estate described on the attached Exhibit A." You can define other terms also, such as "sale price," "closing date," and the like, and then use those terms instead of the specific information. If the parties negotiate a change in the closing date from January 20 to March 4, you can make that change in one place, and one place only, by redefining "closing date," confident that you have made that change through the entire contract.

More to the point, you can use the same form as your base form for another transaction that will close on August 15, simply by changing the definition of "closing date."

Along the same lines, you can use the words "landlord" and "tenant" to refer to the landlord and tenant in a lease, giving the names of the parties only in the beginning of the lease, and then use that lease as a base form for other leases and other properties. I recommend using the words "landlord" and "tenant" instead of the words "lessor" and "lessee" because many clients, and not a few lawyers, get confused between the words "lessor" and "lessee" but always understand the meanings of the words "landlord" and "tenant."

You don't have to wait for clients to come in with specific problems to start building your forms library. Your state or local bar associations likely have forms as part of CLE materials. The section of Real Property, Trust and Estate Law of the American Bar Association puts on many fine CLE programs about real estate sales, leasing, and financing, some of which come with disks or downloads of sample forms that you can then modify for your own use. Don't overlook forms in your state statutes. For example, the legislatures of Oregon and Washington (the states where I'm currently licensed) have passed legislation to adopt statutory deed forms.[1]

If you represent the owner of a multitenant building, you will likely end up developing a base form of lease for that building. If it is a commercial building, tenants will negotiate special provisions for their leases that the owner (your client) might be willing to offer that tenant but does not want to offer other prospective tenants. When you are modifying your form lease, identify those provisions with the words "SPECIAL PROVISION" in bold capitals before each of those paragraphs. If several years later you should use that form as a base for another tenant in the same building, you will recognize those provisions as having been specially negotiated, and you

---

1. Oregon's deed forms are at ORS 93.850 to 93.870. Required notices are also at ORS 93.040, 93.260, and other places. Washington provides deed forms at RCW 64.04.030 to 64.04.050. Many other states have enacted statutory deed forms. New York's are at Section 258 of the Real Property code. California's statutory grant deed form is at Section 1092 of the Civil Code.

can remove them from the form before your client supplies it to the prospective tenant.

You can apply this principle to other fields of law, even those without statutory forms. For example, if you represent landlords, you will eventually be doing evictions; if you develop a landlord-tenant practice, you will also be doing evictions or defending against evictions. Develop a bank of forms for notices to defaulting tenants, for complaints for evictions, and for answers to complaints for evictions.

Now that you have developed a bank of forms to use as bases for other clients, you will need an efficient way to retrieve them. Until you buy document management software, I recommend you organize your forms through a logical folder structure on your computer or server. You should already have a folder or set of folders for each client in each matter. Create a separate folder on your computer for forms, sorted by category of law or in some way that makes sense to you. You need your indexing system to make sense to you or it won't do you any good. Anyone can file documents away (whether in paper files or on a computer), but it takes a good indexing system to be able to find them again.

As I discuss in more detail in Section VI.F.1.3, I have an electronic folder for forms, broken down into 15 or 20 different fields of law, and broken down further within each field. For example, I have a folder labeled "Business" that has subfolders that include "Corporations," "LLCs," and "Limited Partnerships." The folder for LLCs has subfolders for articles of organization, operating agreements, and subscription agreements. I have different folders for articles of organization for different states.

Give your electronic files descriptive names. We are long past the point when filenames were limited to eight letters plus a three letter extension. Electrons are cheap now—use them lavishly when you are naming your files. Be descriptive. For example, I have files indicated as articles of organization for a single member LLC, articles of organization for a two-member friendly LLC, articles of organization for a multimember LLC, articles of organization for a manager-managed LLC, and many others. I abbreviate some of these words, but I include a lot of description in the filename. It will be frustrating to open and go through dozens of files to look for a suitable agreement because you used file names that didn't describe the document well enough to be meaningful to you.

If you install document management software, the software will force you to identify your documents with client name or number, document type, and a title. Document management software will also let you search your files efficiently by client number or title or date. Even if you are starting your practice without document management software, name your files as if you have it in place and so that you tell what is in a file without opening it. If I'm representing Acme Industries in a lease to W. E. Coyote Enterprises, and I'm drafting the lease, I might call the draft that I first send to the tenant's counsel "Lease Acme-Coyote" followed by a code for the date, let's say "Lease Acme-Coyote 7-24-15." When I receive a revision from the tenant's counsel, I might save that as "Lease Acme-Coyote Tenant 8-1-15" to indicate that the tenant's counsel generated it. If I then respond, accepting some changes and rejecting others, I will send a clean version and a redline that shows which of the tenant's changes I've rejected or modified, and I'll name those files something like "Lease Acme-Coyote DNA 8-5-15 CLEAN" and "Lease Acme-Coyote DNA 8-5-15 REDLINE." (My initials are DNA.) When Acme and Coyote have signed the lease, I will scan the signed lease and save the scan as a PDF file called "Lease Acme-Coyote SIGNED."

You can find forms in some unconventional places. Although as a real estate lawyer you are unlikely to need to draft a lot of employment agreements, you can find very sophisticated employment agreements online as exhibits to the proxy statements of public companies. You can download and copy those and adapt them to your own. Other proxy statements may include very complicated pieces. You will rarely need to add anything to them, but they will serve as a checklist of everything that very talented lawyers negotiated for a large project. That, incidentally, is another function that your standard form will serve: a good form is a checklist for the issues to consider in writing a lease, a sale agreement, or another contract. In a long form, every paragraph represents someone's attempt to solve a problem because something was left out of an earlier contract. Some paragraphs represent lawsuits that came out the wrong way.

As your practice grows, you may hire a legal assistant. Your legal assistant will work much more efficiently if you have a forms library from which he or she can start. You can then dictate a memo with the essential points of the transaction, indicate a form to start with, and get back a draft that is

95 percent complete. Of course, as the owner of the firm, you are responsible to your client for the quality of the final product.

Your local legal publishing company will also have forms for sale. Some legal publishing companies will license electronic versions of these forms to lawyers for a period of time or for a particular number of uses. Many simple transactions can be documented on preprinted forms to which you attach a short addendum with specific terms. The preprinted forms can serve as a forms library for you until you develop your own.

Don't be afraid to remove the archaic eighteenth century language from the forms that you collect. Your state has not enacted a statute that requires all contracts to begin with "WITNESSETH." Nor must a contract contain "to-wit" or "hereinbefore" to be enforceable. Revise your forms so that your clients can understand them.

In summary, write your agreements so that they are easy to adapt to other transactions. Devise a clean and effective system to find them again. Don't be bashful at using forms available in the public record or from legal publishing companies. (Respect the copyrights of the publishing companies, however.) For every client who sniffs at you for using the preprinted form, ten others will appreciate that you are saving them money. And for those matters that the preprinted form can't handle, you will have a solid forms library of you own from which to draw.

Chapter XVI

Conflicts With and Between Clients

A. Recognizing Conflicts Between Your Clients

As your practice grows, you will encounter conflicts between your clients. Client A may want to buy a property from Client B. Client C may want to sue Client D. You will of course resolve these conflicts in accordance with the ethical rules of your state bar.

What does it mean to "resolve" a conflict between two clients or prospective clients? (Let's call them E and F here.) It can mean any of several things. First, it might mean that you determine, under your bar's rules, that a conflict between E and F does not in fact exist, and you can take them both on as clients. Second, it might mean that you determine a conflict does exist, but it's one to which Clients E and F can give informed consent. Third, it might mean that you can represent E or F, but not both. Fourth, it might mean that you can't represent even one of E and F.

Let's start with an easy situation, analyzed under Rule 1.7 of the ABA's Model Rules of Professional Conduct.[1] Ms. E wants to hire you to sue Mr. F. Neither E nor F is your client when Ms. E comes to your office. You accept the engagement. When Mr. F finds out, he wants to hire you to negotiate a settlement with Ms. E.

Our starting point is RPC 1.7:

---

1. I'll refer to these as the RPCs.

(a) Except as provided in paragraph (b), a lawyer shall not represent a client if the representation involves a concurrent conflict of interest. A concurrent conflict of interest exists if:

(1) the representation of one client will be directly adverse to another client; or

(2) there is a significant risk that the representation of one or more clients will be materially limited by the lawyer's responsibilities to another client, a former client or a third person or by a personal interest of the lawyer.

(b) Notwithstanding the existence of a concurrent conflict of interest under paragraph (a), a lawyer may represent a client if:

(1) the lawyer reasonably believes that the lawyer will be able to provide competent and diligent representation to each affected client;

(2) the representation is not prohibited by law;

(3) the representation does not involve the assertion of a claim by one client against another client represented by the lawyer in the same litigation or other proceeding before a tribunal; and

(4) each affected client gives informed consent, confirmed in writing.

You cannot represent Mr. F in the lawsuit because that would be directly adverse to your representation of Ms. E, who is already your client, and the representation involves "the assertion of a claim by one client represented by the lawyer in the same litigation or other proceeding before a tribunal."

Most potential conflicts don't show up in such a neat package. Consider this one: Ms. E wants to engage you to advise her in buying Mr. F's property. You helped Mr. F buy the property several years ago, but he hasn't called you since then and you don't consider him to be your client now. Two traps await you here. First is that even though you don't think Mr. F is still your client, he may think you're still his lawyer. Perhaps he hasn't had any legal needs since the time you helped him buy the property. The RPCs don't discuss the point, but state courts have held that it's the client belief that matters: if Mr. F reasonably thinks you're his lawyer based on some objective facts, then you might still be his lawyer, no matter what you think.[2]

Second is that some of your duties to your clients continue even after they stop being your clients. Under RPC 1.9(a):

A lawyer who has formerly represented a client in a matter shall not thereafter represent another person in the same or a substantially related matter in which that person's interests are materially adverse to the interests of the former client unless the former client gives informed consent, confirmed in writing.

Under RPC 1.9(c), the lawyer shall not use information relating to the representation of the former client to the disadvantage of the former client except as permitted by the RPCs, or if the information has become generally known.

You can represent Ms. E in buying Mr. F's property, if Mr. F gives informed consent confirmed in writing. RPC 1.0(e) defines "informed consent," and you should read the definition carefully. "Informed consent" does not simply mean what the plain words say but is defined to be "the agreement by a person to a proposed course of conduct after the lawyer has communicated adequate information and explanation about the material risks of and reasonably available alternatives to the proposed course of conduct."

So if you have telephoned your old friend Mr. F and said jovially, "you don't mind if I represent Ms. E, do you," you have not received informed consent even if Mr. F tells you "Why, yes, I don't mind at all. I'm delighted to have you in the transaction on her side." You have not obtained the informed consent of Mr. F because you have not given Mr. F adequate information and an explanation about the material risks, and you have

---

2. *See*, for example, Westinghouse Elect. Corp. v. Kerr-McGee Corp, 580 F.2d 1311 (7th Cir. 1978) (the client's reasonable subjective belief can be the basis for forming an attorney-client relationship); Lister v. State Bar of California, 51 Cal. 3d 1117, 1126 (1990) (the parties' conduct may imply that an attorney-client relationship exists, even without a fee payment or formal agreement); *compare In re* Weidner, 310 Or. 757, 770 (1990) (a lender who saved money by not hiring his own lawyer did not have an attorney-client relationship with a lawyer who owned an interest in the borrower and who prepared some of the legal documents for a loan from the lender to the borrower and who notarized some of the loan documents).

not given him reasonably available alternatives to your representing Ms. E. Even if you do give Mr. F adequate information and an explanation, and the reasonably available alternatives, and even if he consents to your representing Ms. E after you do all that, the rule requires you to confirm that in writing with Mr. F.

If you do represent Ms. E, you cannot use private information you learned about Mr. F or the property in your representation of Ms. E, unless the information has become generally known. For example, if you learned material nonpublic facts about the property when you helped Mr. F buy the property, you cannot disclose those facts to Ms. E without the permission of Mr. F. However, Mr. F may not want you to disclose those facts. Under those circumstances, you can't represent Ms. E in the transaction. She would expect you to tell her everything important that you know about the property, but your continuing duty to Mr. F prohibits you from disclosing that nonpublic information.

The best way to resolve an impossible situation is to stay out of it.

The discussion of client conflicts could fill a book. This is not that book. This is only a basic discussion of a small portion of the client conflict rules.

B. Recognizing Issue Conflicts; Picking Sides of a General Issue

The first step in resolving client conflicts is to be able to recognize when you have them. For this purpose, you need an efficient and effective client conflict system in which you can enter the names of your clients and their related parties. If you work in a state where lawyers close house purchases and sales, I recommend you also include the property addresses in your conflict system. Although the parties may have had no prior relationship with you, you could conceivably have a conflict of interest if you have had a relationship with a prior owner of a house. You may learn confidential facts about the house that you would be obligated to disclose if another owner became your client. Again, it's best to stay out of the difficult situations rather than to try to solve them once you find yourself in them.

Consider whether you are willing to take on any kind of real estate work, or whether you want to decide in advance whether to limit your practice to one side of a particular kind of case, both to avoid conflicts and to build your reputation in the field. Here are two examples of situations where a little forethought may save you some embarrassment later on.

If you develop a practice representing residential tenants, it's going to be hard to represent a large residential landlord, who from time to time will want to evict some of the people who come to see you as tenants. It may be tempting to accept a residential landlord as a client for one or two matters, but if that representation conflicts you out from taking several cases that you really want to handle, then you haven't helped build your practice.

Along the same lines, if you represent borrowers facing foreclosure, you are going to want to be careful about representing active lenders in the same community who may be suing those borrowers. You run the risk of conflicting yourself out of a line of business you were developing, without any assurance of getting a sufficient flow of business from the clients you hope will replace them.

Your community may have prospective clients who you simply don't want to represent, not because of any fault of the client but because you represent too many other people who do business with them. For instance, in our community, two or three companies control most of the commercial parking business. If you represent owners of office buildings, you may not want to represent the parking companies, even on unrelated matters, because the parking companies will be on the other side of the negotiating table from your office building clients. Similarly, if you develop a practice representing subcontractors who need to file construction liens, you may not want to represent general contractors or landowners who have to defend against those liens.

Likewise, if you have a land use and zoning practice representing clients who apply for permits from the government, consider whether you would take an assignment from a government before which you are presenting land use applications. You would not want your representation of the government agency to conflict you out from advising landowners seeking zoning permits.

C. Identifying Your Client: Do You Represent the Entity or Its Owners?

Having resolved the question of issue conflicts, you now turn to the question of client conflicts. The ideal client, for conflict purposes, is one spouseless, childless, friendless person who owns everything outright, with no entities or co-owners involved. Most clients don't fit that ideal. They own property with a spouse, they give shares in their business entities to their children, and they take on investment partners.

If your client is an entity that has several owners, you will want to be clear with the principals of the entity that the entity is your client.[3] If the owners have different interests, then you will want to be clear that you represent the entity only, and not the individual owners, so that they don't look to you for individual advice on matters that might be adverse to the interests of your actual client. If you represent an entity owned by Bob, Carol, Ted, and Alice, you can't advise Alice on how to force the entity to buy out her share.

If you do represent an entity with several owners, tell the owners in writing that you owe your duty of confidentiality to the entity and not to the individual owners. The individual owners and managers may have conversations with you that are privileged from disclosure to the outside world, but they are not privileged from disclosure to the other members of the entity if they relate to the subject on which you are representing the entity. If one of the members asks you, "You're representing me also, aren't you?," you will need to respond quickly that you are not representing the individual, but only the entity. Or, if you are representing the individual also, you will need to make it clear that you're representing the individual as well as the entity only because their interests don't appear to be in conflict, and that you cannot advise the individual on any matter that is potentially adverse to the entity.

Representing an entity while at the same time representing an individual who is one of several owners of the entity is a delicate exercise, rather like doing ballet on thin ice with an elephant as your dance

---

3. Your engagement letter should always identify your client.

partner. Before you undertake it, consult your state's ethical rules and be sure that you have made all the required disclosures to both the individual and the entity. Stay alert for conflicts that might arise later that would require you to terminate your representation of the individual, the entity, or both.

Chapter XVII

Doing Business with Your Clients

A. Investing with Your Clients—Beware the Thin Ice

Be especially careful of the ethical dangers involved in investing with your clients. Clients who know that you invest in real estate may offer you the opportunity to invest in their projects. You may have the utmost confidence in your client's honesty and ability, and the investment may appear sound. The client may also be your longtime friend. No matter how well you know your client, and no matter how uninvolved you will be in operating the project, you must still follow the steps of Rule 1.8(a) of the Rules of Professional Conduct (RPC) or its equivalent in your state, relating to transacting business with clients. The rule reads:

(a) A lawyer shall not enter into a business relationship with a client or knowingly acquire an ownership, possessory, security or other pecuniary interest adverse to a client unless:

(1) the transaction and terms on which the lawyer acquires the interest are fair and reasonable to the client and are fully disclosed and transmitted in writing in a manner that can be reasonably understood by the client;

(2) the client is advised in writing of the desirability of seeking and is given a reasonable opportunity to seek the advice of independent legal counsel on the transaction; and

(3) the client gives informed consent, in a writing signed by the client, to the essential terms of the transaction and the lawyer's

role in the transaction, including whether the lawyer is representing the client in the transaction.

RPC 1.8(a) is divided into three parts, but actually sets out five conditions that you must fulfill before you invest in your client's project. These conditions follow:

1. The terms of your agreement must be fair to your client.
2. You must disclose the terms of the agreement in writing in a manner that your client can understand.
3. You must recommend to your client in writing that your client seek advice from independent legal counsel on the transaction.
4. Your client must give "informed consent" (a defined term in the RPCs) in writing to the essential terms of the transaction.
5. Your client's informed consent must include a statement about your role, including whether you are representing your client in the transaction.

Even if you aren't representing the client on the particular transaction in which you are investing, the words "your client" in RPC 1.8 include a person whom you represent on some other matter. If you represent Jones in buying Whiteacre, Jones is still "your client" for this rule if you and Jones are investing together in buying Blackacre, even if another lawyer represents Jones, or represents you and Jones, in the Blackacre purchase.

How much disclosure must you make? One authority minces no words: "A lawyer who enters into a business relationship with a client is held to a higher standard than simple arm's length dealing. The lawyer is held to the highest good faith. In approaching the issue of disclosure, the lawyer should acknowledge that he or she is about to undertake a transaction which is presumptively invalid and should remember that he or she will be deemed to occupy a position of superior knowledge and skill and any ambiguities or uncertainties will be construed against the lawyer."[1]

---

1. FRANK A. THOMAS III AND KATHLEEN M. USTON, LAWYERS AND OTHER PEOPLE'S MONEY 26 (5th ed. Virginia State Bar 2012), Section 2.1.

It is not enough to say merely "I recommend that you consult another lawyer." You must also give your client some explanation of the risks of entering into the transaction with you without independent legal advice. Otherwise, if something goes wrong, your client may assert that he was counting on you to provide legal advice and expertise in the transaction.

Farfetched? Consider this actual situation. The lawyer represented a woman in an uncontested divorce. Four years later the woman was sued by a building supply company for the cost of materials furnished to one of her tenants. The lawyer represented her and won the case. The lawyer then learned that his client operated an antiques business and told his client that the lawyer's ex-wife might be interested in being part of the business. The lawyer, his ex-wife, the client, and the client's husband formed a partnership to operate the business. The lawyer wrote articles of partnership, which the four partners signed and filed. The lawyer and his ex-wife contributed $7,500 and the other couple contributed the stock in trade.

The business did not do well, and the partners closed the store a few years later. The lawyer prepared an accounting that showed that the other couple owed him and his ex-wife $3,879, on which the other couple paid $1,300. Two years later, the wife of the other couple called the lawyer for help in separating from her husband. The lawyer said that he could not represent either husband or wife. The wife hired another lawyer and obtained a default decree. A year after that the lawyer handled a real estate sale for the wife. A month later, the husband hired the lawyer to set aside the default, but lost in the trial court, apparently succeeding on appeal. Less than a year later, the lawyer sued the wife for the balance owing on the partnership accounting. The wife tried to bring in her ex-husband as an indispensable party. The couple then agreed to a stipulated judgment against them for the balance. In the meantime, the lawyer filed a dissolution petition on behalf of the husband.[2] The wife then filed a bar complaint.

The Oregon Supreme Court agreed that the partnership agreement prepared by the lawyer contained nothing unusual or unfair and that nothing in the record indicated that the lawyer had overreached or obtained an unfair

2. *In re* Gant, 293 Or. 130, 645 P.2d 23 (1982). It's not at all clear from the published opinion at which times the other couple were married to each other, and at which times they weren't.

advantage. The court did, however, find that the lawyer had violated Canon 5 of the [former] Rules of Professional Conduct and Oregon Disciplinary Rule DR 5-101(A) (similar to today's RPC 1.18) and DR 5-104(A). The court quoted and adopted this finding of the disciplinary panel:

> Although partners in a business anticipate their individual interests will be similar, they can and often do have differing interests. In addition, [the other couple] could well expect the Accused to exercise his professional judgment for their individual protection. The fact that it was possible for the Accused and [the other couple] to have differing interests and also possible [the other couple] expected the Accused to exercise his professional judgment for their individual protection, it was incumbent upon the Accused to advise [wife and husband] to seek independent outside legal advice.

But the first sentence of the court's opinion sums the matter up: "The first charge against the accused attorney involves another instance of the ethical difficulties so frequently encountered when a lawyer enters into a business transaction with a client."

If you do not want to wind up in that lawyer's predicament, then you must take care to follow the requirements of RPC 1.8 in the form adopted by your state. Your letter must identify the conflict, recommend that your client seek independent legal advice, identify at least some of the reasons why your client should seek independent legal advice, and explain your role.

Here is the letter that you might send to Jones to comply with RPC 1.8:

Dear Mr. Jones:

I am writing you this letter in compliance with Rule 1.8 of the Rules of Professional Conduct for lawyers in our state. You have invited me to join you in an investment to buy the Blackacre property, and we have agreed that I will invest $50,000 and own a 30 percent interest with you as a tenant in common.

We have also agreed that your management company will manage and operate the property at the same rates that it charges its other clients, and that we both want to own Blackacre for six to eight years and then sell it if the market is good. We have not agreed on what we will do if you and

I disagree on whether to sell Blackacre, or for how much.

I point out to you that state law gives tenants in common of real property certain rights to force a partition of the property, either as a partition in kind (where the co-owners each receive separate portions of the property), or as a partition and sale (where the property is put up for sale and the proceeds are divided).

RPC 1.8 requires me to make clear what my role is in this transaction. I am advising you on the state of title to the property, the terms of the purchase and sale agreement with the sellers, and the loan documents with the bank that is financing our purchase. I am not advising you, and I cannot advise you, on any agreements between you and me about our purchase and the property itself. I recommend that you seek the advice of independent counsel (neither me nor any of the lawyers in this office) about this transaction, including advice on whether you and I should sign an agreement about how we will make decisions about managing, leasing, financing, and selling Blackacre. These decisions can become sources of major disagreements between us, can be expensive to resolve, and can result in you and I focusing on our disputes instead of on running Blackacre profitably.

I am not giving you any tax advice about this purchase, and I recommend that you consult your tax attorney or accountant about the tax aspects.

If you agree with my description of our transaction, please sign a copy of this letter and return it to me. A fax or scan is fine.
Very truly yours,

Pruden T. Lawyer

I have read your letter. The terms of the letter are fair and reasonable to me and I understand them. I acknowledge that you have advised me to seek the advice of independent legal counsel. I have had a reasonable opportunity to consult another lawyer, and I have either consulted another lawyer about this transaction or have decided not to.
John Q. Client
May ____, 20____.

RPC 1.8 applies even if you are only one of several investors in your client's project, and even if you don't expect to have any voice in the project. Let's suppose that your client is a real estate syndicator, that you do the client's syndication work, and that you want to invest in one of your client's projects, in which you would be one of ten outside investors. In this circumstance, you've already written a form of syndication agreement, co-tenancy agreement, or management agreement for other projects of your client. Even though you aren't going to negotiate the agreement with your client as you might if you were the only other investor, you must still give the RPC 1.8 disclosure.

You should also be clear that you don't represent the other investors because if they learn that a lawyer is one of the investors, they might believe that the lawyer (you) will look out for their legal interests also.

Here is the letter you might send to your client:

Dear Mr. Jones:

I am writing you this letter in compliance with Rule 1.8 of the Rules of Professional Conduct for lawyers in our state. You have invited me to become one of the limited partners in your company's acquisition of the Greenacre property, in which you are offering 40 limited partnership interests for $10,000 per unit. I plan to buy five units for a total investment of $50,000.

As you know, I have represented you and your company on other purchases in which you've solicited outside investors to become limited partners, and you plan to use the same form of subscription agreement, partnership agreement, and investor disclosures that I drafted for your other projects, modified only as necessary to apply to Greenacre.

RPC 1.8 requires me to make clear what my role is in this transaction. I am advising you and your company on the state of title to the property, the terms of the purchase and sale agreement with the sellers, the loan documents with the bank that is financing our purchase, and the proper documentation of the subscriptions you are receiving from the other investors. I am not advising you, and I cannot advise you, on any agreements between you and me about our purchase and the property itself. I recommend that you seek the advice of independent counsel (neither me nor any of the lawyers in this office) about this transaction.

I also want to be clear that I don't represent the other limited partners. They are not my clients in this project, and I am not their lawyer. The only advice I can give them is to recommend that they consult their own lawyers about the partnership and the project.

If you agree with my description of our transaction, please sign a copy of this letter and return it to me. A fax or scan is fine.

Very truly yours,

Pruden T. Lawyer

I have read your letter. The terms of the letter are fair and reasonable to me, and I understand them. I acknowledge that you have advised me to seek the advice of independent legal counsel. I have had a reasonable opportunity to consult another lawyer, and I have either consulted another lawyer about this transaction or have decided not to.
John Q. Client
Client Enterprises, Inc.
May ____, 20___.

B. Investing *for* Your Clients: Beware the Even Thinner Ice

An easier danger to spot, and a deeper pitfall if you succumb to it, is the temptation to solicit a client to invest with you in a project that you will run, whether it be an apartment house in your hometown or a fish farm in a foreign country. When you invest your client's money with your own, you set up at least two future conflicts. If you charge the enterprise for your legal work, your client—who is now your coinvestor also—may object to the amount and nature of your legal fees. Your client may say that the work you're charging a legal fee for is part of your duties as a co-owner, and that it's not fair for you to charge for what you should be doing anyway as a co-owner. The result may be that your client becomes a former client and files a complaint with your state bar.

This actual case contains most of these elements: a lawyer represented Client A on several matters. The lawyer began to represent Client B in a caviar production and distribution business, conducted through several related corporations. The lawyer eventually stopped taking new clients and spent most of his time as legal counsel to Client B and the caviar project, though he kept Client A and a few others as clients.

The lawyer told Client A about the caviar project, and Client A gave him $65,000 to invest in the caviar project, expecting to receive stock in one of the caviar corporations. The lawyer did not tell Client A that the caviar project employed him and did not disclose the conflicts of interest or get written waivers from Client A and Client B.

The lawyer disbursed $25,000 to one of the caviar corporations, $20,000 to Client B, and $20,000 to himself for legal fees on the caviar project, which was not how Client A expected his money to be used. The lawyer later became a shareholder in one of the caviar corporations. The lawyer tried to have Client B acknowledge that Client A had contributed $65,000 in capital to one of the corporations, but Client B refused.

Client A then demanded his money back. The lawyer prepared a promissory note for the money (apparently a note from the lawyer to Client A, not from the caviar corporations) and agreed to represent Client A to recover the money from Client B. As a result of this conflict and other unwaived conflicts, the state bar suspended the lawyer's license for two years.[3]

C. How and When to Do Business with Your Clients

Don't take the preceding sections as my warnings never to do business with your clients. You should do business with clients whenever you can—by purchasing from their businesses and using their services.

We lease our office space from one of our clients. I bought my house through a real estate agent that I represented and closed the escrow with a title company client. I am proud to drive a car that I bought from an automobile dealer that I represent, to take friends out to eat at a restaurant whose lease I negotiated, to vacation at a resort whose land use permits I obtained, and to buy tickets to the games of a sports team that I advised. One of my goals for my clients is to increase their gross revenue, both by my advice and with my business.

A lawyer friend who also represented a car dealer bought a new car of a brand that the dealer sold, but he bought it from a different dealer, one that he didn't represent. He explained that he would have been embarrassed to ask his dealer client for a discount, and so he went to the other dealer. To my mind the dealer would be more offended by learning that

---

3. *In re* Ordinartsev, Washington State Bar Association (Nov. 29, 2004).

his lawyer bought his car from the competitor than if his lawyer asked the salesman for a discount.

In the same situation, I would not ask the dealer for a discount, nor would I expect one. I bought my car from a salesman who did not know that I represented the dealership. He quoted a fair price for the car I bought and a fair price for the car that I traded in. Only after we signed the contracts did I mention that I knew (and represented) the owner. I then wrote the owner a note about the fine professional service I'd received from his salesman.

I have occasionally asked a client for a favor (such as help getting a gift to a guest at a resort, for which I paid), but never for a discount or a price break. Nor should you. Your clients are some of the finest people in your community, for they've entrusted you with their affairs. If they pay your fees promptly and agree that your services are worth what you charge, why would you suggest that you don't think their products and services are worth what they charge?

Chapter XVIII

Growing Your Practice

A. Investing in the Support Structure to Grow

If you are building your real estate practice at a firm, then the management of the firm will be setting the goals for your practice. If you are building your real estate practice as a solo or at a firm that you would help start, then you will enjoy the luxury of setting your own goals.

If your goal is to make a reasonable living, then you may be content with being a solo operator. If you would like to grow your practice to the point where you can hire law clerks and associates, then you should start your practice with that in mind.

If you are starting your practice on more than a shoestring, make your technology purchases with the view toward growing your office. For example, buy a telephone system with the extra capacity to handle more users. Buy a network server one or two sizes larger than what you need, so that it can accommodate more users in the future. Obtain an Internet domain name for your firm so that you and your future coworkers can have e-mail addresses associated with your firm, and not a generic Yahoo, Hotmail, or Gmail address. When I started my firm as a solo, I bought telephone and network equipment that could serve 16 users, even though at the start I had just four.

As Chapter VI discusses, organize your forms library to be as efficient as possible so that you can quickly train an associate or a law clerk to prepare documents based on your forms. If while you are a solo you don't organize your work so that you can find it again, then when you do hire an associate, your associate will waste a lot of time searching for base forms, and you will waste a lot of time helping your associate find your base forms and other client information.

B. Growing by Hiring

One reason to train a law clerk or associate is so that you can occasionally take a vacation, or have the office covered if you should become ill. Another reason is that when two clients bring urgent projects at the same time, it's convenient to have two people available to work on them. A third reason is that all but the least gregarious among us would rather spend our day in an office that has other people in it.

Assuming that you would like to expand your office and your practice, evaluate the work you do and determine, as coldly and honestly as possible, how much of it requires a person with your education and expertise to do, and how much could be accomplished by a reasonably intelligent person with some training. In other words, consider how much of your work you could delegate downward if you have staff available. For some of us, our work really is akin to brain surgery in the sense that we do something so specialized that we cannot easily train another person to do it. That portion of our daily work is much less than we like to think it is. The great skill we learn in law school is to spot issues, and it takes several years of education followed by several years of practical experience to be able to do it well. It takes less skill, however, to examine case law and statutes to confirm that the legal principles that apply to a certain situation are still the same as they were when we learned them in law school, and it takes rather less skill (but much more attention to detail) to prepare a trust deed in a format that the county recorder will accept.

The time to hire an associate is before you are so totally overwhelmed that you can't accomplish anything at the office. For the first few weeks or months, either you or the associate will be underworked. Don't let that scare you. Delegate as much as possible of your work to your associate, and train the associate to do it. Start by giving your associate specific tasks to do, and then move him or her to larger sections of matters and then eventually to entire matters. You can then use your extra time to work on matters that require more experience, to build your network of referral sources, to contribute time and expertise to the local bar association, or to be with your family.

It's a general principle of management that work should be delegated downward to the least experienced person who is qualified to do it. Your goal should be to give your associate all the work in the office that your associate is qualified to do and then to train your associate to be able to do more of the work that you are now doing yourself.

"Training" by itself is an amorphous concept. If you set out to train your associate but you don't identify your objective, you and your associate are both going to be disappointed by the result.

"Training" your associate doesn't mean that you have to become a classroom teacher. You can train your associate effectively if you will adopt a list of skills that you want your associate to have, and then set about giving your associate the opportunities to develop those skills, coupled with your evaluation on how the associate has done and how the associate can produce better work.

Here is a list of skills that you might want your associate to develop:

- Evaluate a title report;
- Read loan documents for conformance to a commitment letter;
- Draft a promissory note and trust deed to conform to a term sheet;
- Write an access easement;
- Check and confirm legal descriptions;
- Handle a commercial eviction;
- Form LLCs in [home state] and Delaware;
- Get zoning information from local jurisdictions; and
- Write an application for a variance.

Share your list with your associate. If your associate knows what skills you want to teach, he or she is more likely to learn those skills.

When you've written your list, look for projects on which your associate can learn these skills, and assign parts of those projects to your associate. Keep track on your list of the projects you've given your associate. After a few months your list of skills, with your annotations that identify what projects the associate has worked on, might look like this:

- Evaluate a title report
  - Acme apartment purchase, noted conflicting easements
  - Beta sale, obtained releases of the easements
- Read loan documents for conformance to a commitment letter
  - Acme loan, handled well
- Draft a promissory note and trust deed to conform to a term sheet
  - Beta seller carryback, need to explain amortization
- Write an access easement
- Check and confirm legal descriptions
  - Acme purchase, handled well
  - Beta sale, handled well
- Handle a commercial eviction
- Form LLCs in [home state] and Delaware
  - Acme purchase, formed buying LLC
  - Charlie purchase, formed buying LLC
- Get zoning information from local jurisdictions
  - Acme purchase due diligence, Centerville Planning Authority
  - Charlie purchase, Northton zoning department
- Write an application for a variance

Six months after you've hired your associate, review your list and your annotations with your associate. You may find that you've given your associate a lot of experience in a few areas and not so much in others. In the example I've given here, the associate has handled a lot of tasks involving research and evaluation, but only a few tasks that involved writing documents. The employing attorney (you) might look at the list of tasks accomplished, see that the associate has not drafted many agreements, and focus the next six months on developing the associate's skills at drafting agreements.

Your associate may also have developed a taste for work in some areas and not others. Modify your training program as necessary to suit what you need and what your associate likes to work on.

Invest the time to review your associate's work and explain what you like and what you don't like. When you're sharing your evaluation and suggestions with your associate, be clear about what you would have done differently. You can tell your associate, "I don't like how you handled the use clauses because you have the prohibited uses in three different places in the lease, instead of making one group of uses that are prohibited because other tenants have exclusives on them, and another group of uses that our client doesn't allow anywhere in the center" which is more useful feedback than if you tell your associate only, "You made a mess of the use clause." Both statements express that you are unhappy, but only the first statement adds to your associate's training by suggesting how he or she can do better work the next time.

If you practice in a city with a law school, an easy and inexpensive way to augment your practice is to hire a law clerk from among the first- and second-year students at the law school. You may not need a full-time person, and the law student may be able to work less than fulltime. The law clerk will appreciate the experience, and you'll appreciate having someone to do the tasks that take you away from your most valuable and productive work. Pick someone who wants to stay in town after graduation; the right law clerk can make a smooth transition after graduation to being your associate.

C. Growing by Partnership

A more difficult step is deciding whether to go into partnership with another lawyer. A partnership with a lawyer you like is a good way to spread the risk of opening a new practice. A partnership with the wrong person is a good way to turn a friend into a plaintiff when the partnership breaks up. Lawyers form partnerships for all sorts of reasons, and I can't begin to list them all here. To my mind, forming a law partnership makes sense when you and your partner bring complementary strengths to the partnership. For instance, if you like office work and your partner wants to litigate, then a partnership makes sense if your partner is willing to litigate real estate matters. You can then handle real estate transactions and your partner can litigate real estate disputes, which will help build your firm's reputation as an expert in real estate matters. On the other hand, if you want to practice real estate and your partner wants to practice personal injury law, there won't be a lot of opportunity for you to refer clients to your partner or your partner to refer clients to you. You may be very compatible people, but your practices are not. A better arrangement in that situation is to share space and some of the costs of running an office without forming a business partnership.

Some space-sharing arrangements work out very well. I know a white-collar criminal defense attorney who rented space from a firm with a strong business and civil litigation practice. The white-collar criminal defendants often had business needs, or became enmeshed in civil litigation outside the defense attorney's practice, and he could easily refer them to the lawyers down the hall. Similarly, when clients of the business attorneys needed advice on federal criminal matters and income tax investigations, the business attorneys could easily refer those clients to the defense attorney. That office-sharing arrangement has lasted for more than 40 years.

If you do decide to form a partnership, discuss your goals for your practice with your prospective partner before signing on. If one of you wishes to make as much money as possible and the other one wants to provide a public service, your partnership will likely break up when one partner looks at the overhead and the other partner looks at the income.

Check out your prospective partner's reputation and sense of ethics before agreeing to go into business together. Don't wait until the paint dries on your office door to find out your partner's reputation in the legal community. When you form a partnership, your ethics and reputation become your partner's, and your partner's ethics and reputation become yours.

Another consideration in going into partnership should be the future plans of you and your partner. Do you both intend to practice about the same length of time? In that case, unless you expect simply to close your office when you both retire, you will need at some point to plan to hire associates to whom you can transition your clients, or to transfer your files to a larger firm. If your partner is much older or much younger than you, come to an agreement about whether part of the goal of the partnership is for the older partner to transfer his or her clients to the younger partner on retirement.

A strong reason to seek out a partnership is if your practice depends entirely on one client. If you can form a partnership with two or three other lawyers in related practice areas, then you can have a firm in which the large client is only 25 percent of the billings instead of 100 percent of the billings. You will still lie awake at night and worry about losing the client, but you can also spread the client's work around among other lawyers and make some time for yourself to market your services and broaden your client base.

Chapter XIX

Transitioning Your Practice; Preparing for Retirement

A. Planning Your Practice for Transition and Retirement

Next, think about your own retirement plan and schedule. If your practice has steady clients, then look for a partner or an associate who will be able to pick up and service your clients when you retire. I knew a lawyer who practiced until he was 99. He transitioned his clients to his son, who was 67. His was not the typical retirement plan, and it's unlikely to be yours. More likely, you may want to work until you are somewhere between 60 and 75, with your actual age at retirement dependent on factors such as your health, your savings and investments, and your financial obligations—not just mortgages and business debt but also commitments for college tuition for your children and support of other relatives.

Your transition plan should have two parts: planning what will happen to your practice (the practice planning) and planning your own financial future (the financial planning). You don't need to have these fully worked out when you start your practice, but you should have your general financial plan in mind when you start your practice, and you should start to work on your practice planning about 10 years before you intend to retire.

Modern changes in ethical rules have opened up new options for lawyers who are planning for retirement. It used to be that lawyers could not buy or sell law practices. The comment to Rule 1.17 of the ABA's Model Rules of Professional Conduct (RPCs), adopted by most states, explains the reason behind the traditional rule in these words: "The practice of law is a profession, not merely a business. Clients are not commodities that can be purchased or sold at will." Despite its statement of the traditional rule, RPC 1.17 does allow a lawyer to sell an entire law practice, or an entire practice area, in much the same way that physicians and dentists buy and sell practices. RPC 1.17 imposes several conditions on a lawyer's sale of a law practice, which include a requirement to give affected clients a written notice of the sale and to allow clients 90 days to object to transferring files from the selling lawyer to the buying lawyer.

Whether you can sell your practice will depend not just on how well your practice performs financially (i.e., on how much money you are making) but on the nature of your clients. If your practice succeeds and your clients come to you because of your location (e.g., if you are one of a very few lawyers in a small town or suburb), you can sell it to a buyer who expects that new clients will continue to come to the location and current clients will stay because of the location.[1]

If most of your work comes from repeat clients, some of your clients will trust your judgment in choosing a successor to carry on your practice. Comment 11 to RPC 1.17 is a reminder that if you sell your practice, you are subject to the same ethical rules that govern whether and how you can involve another lawyer in representing your client. One of these obligations is "to exercise competence in identifying a purchaser qualified to assume the practice," meaning that you can sell your practice only to a lawyer whom you reasonably believe is competent to handle the work that your clients will bring. If your practice consists entirely of negotiating and drafting retail leases, you can't ethically sell it to a lawyer with no real estate experience who has handled only divorces.

It's more difficult to sell your practice if most of your clients come for one engagement only, or if your practice is relatively undifferentiated from those of the other lawyers in your area. In that case, your transition plan may be to find a younger lawyer with some experience in your practice

---

1. This situation of clients being passed from one practitioner to another on the sale of a business is more common in health care than in law. For 46 years I've gone to the same dental practice, which has been sold twice by retiring dentists since my first visit, but it is still in the same building as it was in 1968 when I first went there.

area, or who is willing to learn it, whom you can envision as your partner in a year or two. Over several years you would then introduce the lawyer to your clients and involve the lawyer in your work. When your transition period is complete you would then retire, with the younger lawyer's agreement to pay you a retirement benefit for the goodwill of the practice over a period of time.

A third way to move toward retirement is to merge your practice into another law firm, with the object of transitioning your clients to the other lawyers in the firm. Whether the merger will be governed by RPC 1.17 will depend on how you design it: if you sell your practice to the larger firm, then RPC 1.17 requires you to retire. If you merge your practice into the larger firm without selling it, then RPC 1.17 does not cover your agreement. You're still subject to the other rules for professional conduct in your jurisdiction.

B. Planning Your Finances for Retirement

An important part of your retirement plan is your retirement planning, meaning your savings and investment program to accumulate funds to be able to retire. Start a tax-deferred retirement plan, such as a 401(k), an individual retirement account, or other savings mechanism so that you will be able to retire when you want to. The best plan to transition your work to the people coming along after you will fail if you can't afford to retire when you want to retire, or when a health crisis suddenly forces you to retire.

This portion of your plan can be summarized in a few words as "Save enough money; invest it well; reinvest the income." Beyond these few words lie an opportunity and some dangerous temptations.

The opportunity is that your practice will teach you a lot about how to invest in real estate. As you assist your clients in buying and managing apartments, retail centers, or office buildings, you will learn something of how to choose, manage, finance, and sell the same kinds of properties. You will also develop relationships with real estate brokers who will send you e-mails and flyers about the properties that they offer for sale. You will have chances to buy investment real estate that many people won't see, and wise choices of property can form a large part of your retirement fund.

With this opportunity come some dangerous temptations. One of these is that if you are an active buyer of real estate of the type that your clients buy, your clients may start to see you as a competitor. You won't have a big problem if you are buying duplexes and small apartment buildings—all but the smallest of cities have a large supply, so you are not taking opportunities away from your clients—but it can become an irritation to your clients if you are buying larger properties, or if you are buying nonresidential properties and competing with your clients for the same tenants. I don't know how you would explain to your client that even though your client's tenant is moving from its storefront in your client's building to a similar storefront in your building, you didn't use any facts from your client when you negotiated the new lease with the tenant. I do know that whatever your explanation may be, your client may not believe it, and may think that you had unethically used information about your client for your own financial gain.

The ethical traps of another danger, investing with your clients, are covered in Section XVII.A. It suffices here to say that if you do invest with clients, read and comply with your state's version of RPC 1.8.

C. Planning for the Unplanned Transition: Death and Disability

Part of planning is to plan for the unexpected. You can project a retirement date and direct your financial planning toward that goal, even if you should later choose to stay in practice a few years longer, whether to handle a challenging project or to give your retirement fund time to recover from a recession. But what if you have an unplanned retirement? I'm speaking of death and disability, and I will assume that you have dependents—family members who would be financially strapped if you were to die and your income stopped.

Until you have built an estate that will support your family and provide tuition for your children, the simplest and cheapest way to protect your family against your early death is to buy term life insurance. The amount of insurance that you need to provide support for your family is a matter to discuss with your financial advisor and your insurance agent. In addition to that insurance, consider what your survivors will spend to wind up your practice if you die suddenly. You may have borrowed from a bank to finance your start-up cost. You may have financed the tenant improvements and furniture in your office. You may have years left on your office lease and equipment leases. The administrator of your estate will need to pay off your business debts and may need to buy out the remaining term of your office lease and equipment leases, or keep paying the rent until he or she can find a subtenant. Your staff will have to be paid to stay, move files to other lawyers, and wind up your practice. These obligations should be part of your life insurance planning.

If you are a solo practitioner, then you should also have an emergency plan for your clients to receive at least some attention from another lawyer if you should die unexpectedly. Two solo practitioners can agree that if one should die or become seriously disabled, the other will step in and manage the caseload. If you make this agreement with a colleague, you will need to leave the colleague instructions on what to do in your office regarding: what systems you use, how you arrange your files, where copies of your leases are, what your docketing system is, and so on. You do not have to give your colleague that information now, but you must write it down and keep it in your office where your staff can find it and give it to the second lawyer.

A very simple step is to maintain a current case list, a list of your active files and matters with a short description of the matter. Litigators maintain case lists; transactional lawyers should copy the habit. Even though I practice in a firm, I maintain a list of my active matters and update it every week. If I die or become so ill that I can't work, my partners and associates can go through the list and make sure that none of my clients' matters is forgotten.

Of nearly equal importance is considering what will happen to your practice and your finances if you become temporarily or permanently disabled. You can buy disability insurance to replace a portion of your income if you are permanently disabled to the point where you cannot practice law. The typical long-term disability policy pays a benefit that starts X days after you become disabled (30, 60, 90, or 180 days) and continues until you are 65 years old. Short-term disability insurance is also available: a typical policy might start to pay a monthly benefit 30 days after you become disabled and will continue for up to 1 year. Whether you practice by yourself or with others, having some disability insurance will provide you and your family with an assurance of income if you can no longer work.

A disability insurance policy can be written as "own occupation" or "any occupation." An "own occupation" policy pays the benefit if you are disabled to the point that you cannot work at your usual occupation (i.e., if you can no longer work as a lawyer). An "any occupation" policy is cheaper but has a more restrictive definition of being disabled: you are disabled if you can't work at any occupation. The "own occupation" policy is a superior product for lawyers because of the strong chance that a disabled lawyer who can still work at some other job won't be able to earn as much from that job as from practicing law.

The insurer will examine your tax returns and income statement in determining how much coverage to provide. The insurer does not want to offer you so much coverage that you have a financial incentive to become disabled and stop working; the coverage is intended to replace your income, not to augment it. If you buy the coverage with after-tax dollars then the benefit comes to you free of income tax, meaning that if you pay 40 percent of your income in income taxes, a disability policy that replaces 60 percent of your income will put you in the same after-tax situation as you are now.

You can also buy a short-term disability insurance policy to cover your office overhead expenses for a shorter period, usually up to one year. If you suffer a short-term disability and can't work for six months, you may nevertheless want to keep your office open and staff employed so that when you are ready to come back to work, your staff and office will still be there. The insurer examines your office overhead and financial statements to determine how much coverage to offer, except that in this instance the carrier seeks not to replace your income but to cover your out-of-pocket expenses. The coverage is limited on the theory that if you can't work for more than one year, you will have closed your office or sold your practice, and you won't have any overhead expenses to cover. The range of disability policies is wide, and you should consult an experienced agent for an explanation of the varieties of coverage.

Chapter XX

Conclusion

The business of law in the United States is undergoing great change, and the changes are accelerating. A century ago, the American bar comprised almost entirely white males, who numbered more than 99 percent of the bar. Today bar membership is more diverse than ever before, and its diversity continues to increase. Half a century ago, lawyers did not advertise. Today you can see or hear the advertisements of lawyers on radio and television, in newspapers, and on the Internet. Only in recent years has it been considered ethical to buy and sell a law practice, and many nations (and also the District of Columbia, though not yet any of the 50 states) allow nonlawyers to own interests in law firms.

It has been less than 125 years since the National Conference of Commissioners on Uniform State Laws (now simply the Uniform Law Commission) proposed its first uniform act for the states to adopt. Its proposals for uniform laws on real estate include the Uniform Common Interest Ownership Act, the Uniform Condominium Act, the Uniform Conservation Easement Act, and the Uniform Land Transactions Act, among many others. None of these has yet matched the Uniform Commercial Code in popularity, and a few have been adopted by only one or two states. Real estate law remains firmly local, and as long as it remains firmly local, it will always be possible for talented and energetic practitioners to develop a reputation as a real estate lawyer in their communities, and even statewide.

"Under all is the land," begins the preamble of the Code of Ethics of the National Association of Realtors. One hundred years from now, under all the land will still be. And as long as the land is still there and Americans are buying, selling, leasing, zoning, fencing, and improving it, there will be satisfying opportunities for real estate attorneys to open and build law practices.

I hope that you've found this book useful, and I wish you a long and happy career in our profession.

Appendixes

1. Sample Annotated Engagement Letter with Alternate Clauses
2. New Business Form
3. Sample Disengagement Letter
4. Recommended Additional Reading

Appendix 1

Sample Annotated Engagement Letter with Alternate Clauses

The following is a detailed engagement letter for a new client.

(date)
Morrison and Charlotte Horner
Horner Family LLC
1234 Wiley Place
Somewhere, Oregon
Re: TransitCorp condemnation

Dear Mr. and Mrs. Horner:

Thank you for asking us to represent Horner Family LLC in TransitCorp's proposed condemnation of the property at Main Street for the Main Street transit terminal. We appreciate the chance to be of service.

This letter sets out the basic terms of our engagement. I've divided it into sections for ease of reference.

Our Client[1]

Horner Family LLC, a limited liability company of which I understand you are the sole members, is our client for this engagement. We will treat instructions from either of you as being instructions of Horner Family LLC.[2] In other

---

1. A good engagement letter will make it clear whether an individual or an entity is the client. In this letter, I'm stating that the LLC is my client.
2. When an entity hires me, I want to identify the persons from whom I will take instructions on behalf of the entity. This sentence means that until I find out about an actual disagreement between Morrison and Charlotte, I don't have to check with both of them before acting on behalf of Horner Family LLC, but can accept instructions from one.

parts of this letter, "you" and "your" refers to Horner Family LLC unless the context requires it to mean you individually.

Scope of Our Engagement

The scope of this engagement is to negotiate with TransitCorp on the purchase price of your property at Main Street, which TransitCorp wishes to condemn for a public transit project, and to defend the condemnation in court if negotiations are not successful.[3]

Our Fees and Invoices

We usually figure our fees based on the hours we work on your behalf.[4] My current hourly rate is $X. Other lawyers in the firm have rates that range from $Y to $Z. When our staff act as legal assistants (i.e., performing work typically done by legal assistants that goes beyond the merely clerical), we charge $W per hour for their time. Our hourly rates are subject to change, which I expect to do at the beginning of each year.[5] The hourly rates we charge will be those in effect when we do the work. We will ordinarily send you invoices monthly and payment is due to our office within 30 days.

You have the right at any time to terminate our services, but you will still be responsible to pay for the services we rendered and expenses we paid or incurred on your behalf before the date of termination, or in connection with the termination (as, for example, if we provide services or incur expenses in the course of transferring the matter to successor counsel).

We reserve the right to withdraw from this representation if, among other things, you do not honor the terms of the engagement letter or representation and fee agreement,[6] or if any circumstance arises which would or could, in our view, render our continuing representation unlawful or unethical. If we elect to withdraw, we will be entitled to be paid for all services rendered and costs and expenses paid or incurred on your behalf to the date of withdrawal.

---

3. Always describe what you're being hired to do so that the client doesn't later say that you did too much work (for which the client doesn't want to pay you) or too little work (leaving the client exposed to liability for which the client wants you or your insurance carrier to be responsible). This description of the scope of the engagement identifies two specific tasks: (1) negotiate and (2) litigate. It does not include giving advice on other matters related to the condemnation, such as tax consequences, environmental questions, and dealing with tenants of the property.

4. This sentence states that my fee is based on my ordinary hourly rate, but is not a commitment that my fee will always be hours times rate.

5. If you state your hourly rate in your engagement letter, reserve the right to change the rate from time to time. If you state that you will charge $X/hour for the engagement and the engagement lasts for several years, and you haven't reserved the right to increase your rates, then you will be locked into that rate for the life of the engagement.

6. I'm saying in a polite way that I have the right to stop work if the client stops paying my invoices.

Our Costs and Disbursements

We will bill our costs and disbursements to you with a reasonable explanation of what they are and who we paid. "Costs and disbursements" means money that we pay to third parties on your behalf or as part of representing and advising you. In business matters, these include recording fees, fees charged by agencies for copies of public records, travel costs, parking costs (if we drive somewhere on your behalf), delivery fees charged by courier services such as Transerv, FedEx, DHL, and the like.

We do not charge you for routine postage.[7] Those costs are part of our overhead. If we send things by certified or registered mail, or if we have to do a mass mailing for you, then we will charge the actual cost of the postage. Similarly, we do not charge you by the page for routine copying in our office.[8] Those costs are also part of our overhead. If we send a large copying job to an outside service, then we charge you what the service charges us. If we do a large copying job for you in-house (for instance, if we're making copies of long loan or lease documents), we may charge you the same rate per copy that an outside vendor would charge us.

Our long distance telephone vendor charges us 5 cents per minute for domestic long distance. Because that rate is so low, we do not bill you for telephone tolls for domestic long distance. Our international long distance rates are higher, and we bill international long distance at our actual cost. If in the future we can't get domestic long distance at this low cost, we may charge telephone tolls for domestic long distance at our actual cost.

Disputes

If any dispute arises about our fees and charges, the law of the state of Oregon shall apply, and the fee dispute shall be resolved by binding arbitration pursuant to the Oregon State Bar fee dispute program.[9]

File Retention

When our engagement on any matter is completed, we will close the file and return to you original documents that we obtained from you. We do not keep closed files indefinitely and will destroy our file on this matter ten years after we close the file, unless we determine a shorter period to be appropriate.[10]

---

7. Many firms charge for postage, sometimes offending their clients who don't cavil at paying a large fee, but object to being asked to pay a few cents extra for what in their own businesses is simply part of the cost of doing business.

8. As I do with postage, I look on copying as part of my overhead.

9. If your state bar has a fee arbitration program, offer to settle fee disputes through the program.

10. I tell the client in the engagement letter that I will not be his file repository and off-site document storage provider forever.

Other Engagements

If you engage us to do other work for you, the terms of this letter will govern those engagements unless we send you a separate engagement letter for the other work that contains different terms.[11] The terms of that separate engagement letter will apply to that engagement and will prevail over any inconsistent terms in this letter.

To indicate that you accept these terms, please sign and return a copy of this letter to us. A faxed (503-555-1212) or e-mailed (lawyer@samplelawfirm.com) copy is fine. Thank you for asking us to advise Horner Family LLC on this matter.

Very truly yours,

SAMPLE LAW FIRM LLP
Robert J. Sample
ACCEPTED:[12]
Horner Family LLC:
Morrison Horner, Member   Charlotte Horner, Member
November ____, 20___   November ____, 20___
* * * * *

Alternate Clauses for the Sample Engagement Letter

Identifying a Couple as Your Clients

You are our clients for this engagement. Until you tell us of a disagreement between you, we will treat instructions from either of you as being instructions from both of you. Because you will both be our clients, communications between either of you and our office may be privileged against disclosure to third parties, but are not privileged as between you, and if

---

11.   You may not want to send an engagement letter for each matter to a client who hires you steadily for a succession of small matters. This clause says that the general terms of this letter will apply to future engagements unless you send a specific engagement letter with different terms. For example, if I've sent this engagement letter to a new client to take on an hourly matter, and then later on propose to handle a new matter with a contingent fee, a flat fee, or a success fee, I will send an engagement letter for that matter that describes the specific fee agreement for that matter and will state that the fee agreement applies to that matter only.
12.   Provide a space for your clients to sign to indicate that they have read and approved the terms of the engagement and are hiring you.

a disagreement develops between you about this engagement, the ethical rules applicable to lawyers may require me to resign from representing one or both of you.

Identifying an Association or Committee as Your Client

Asphalt Heights Owners Association is our client for this engagement. We will treat instructions from its president (currently Charles Solomon) or its vice president (currently Augusta Kief) as being instructions of the association. We do not represent the directors or the individual home-owners in this engagement. If we receive conflicting instructions, then we reserve the right to suspend work until we receive definitive instructions from the association.

For a Flat Fee

Our fee for this project will be $2,500, payable as $1,250 before we start work and $1,250 when we complete the project and the sale has closed. The initial $1,250 is earned when paid. [Alternate: We will keep the initial $1,250 in our trust account until we send you a first draft of the lease, which is when we will have earned it.] In addition, you will reimburse us for our out-of-pocket costs to third parties.

For a Flat Fee with Milestones

Our fee for this project will be $7,500, payable as $1,500 when we deliver the first draft of the sale agreement, $2,500 when the sale agreement is signed, and $3,500 at closing or when it becomes clear after a sale agreement is signed that the sale will not close. Our fee does not include any charge for handling disputes over the earnest money if the sale does not close, nor for handling any post-closing matters, all of which we will charge at our ordinary hourly rates. In addition, you will reimburse us for our out-of-pocket costs to third parties.

For an Hourly Fee with a Success Fee

Our fee for this engagement has two components, an hourly fee and a success fee. We will figure the hourly portion of our fee based on the hours we work on your behalf. My current hourly rate is $X. Other lawyers in the firm have rates that range from $Y to $Z. When our staff act as legal assistants (i.e., performing work typically done by legal assistants that goes beyond the merely clerical), we charge $W per hour for their time. Our hourly rates are subject to change, which I expect to do at the beginning of each year. The hourly rates we charge will be those in effect when we do the work. We will ordinarily send you invoices monthly, and payment is due to our office within 30 days.

The success portion of the fee will be based on the result that we achieve for you and is 10 percent of the amount by which the price that TransitCorp pays for your property exceeds $2,000,000. For example, if TransitCorp pays you $2,400,000 for your property, then the success portion of our fee will be $40,000 (10 percent of the amount over $2,000,000). This is in addition to our hourly fee and not in place of it. If TransitCorp pays you $2,000,000 or less for your property, then the success portion of the fee will be zero. Whether or not we earn a success fee, you will reimburse us for our out-of-pocket costs to third parties.

Appendix 2

New Business Form

NEW BUSINESS FORM

DATE: _____   Office Phone: _____

Client Name: _____   Cell Phone: _____

Client Number: _____   Home Phone: _____

Matter Number: _____   Facsimile: _____

Address: _____   E-mail: _____

_____   Engagement Letter sent by: _____

_____   Introducing Lawyer: _____

_____   Responsible Lawyer: _____

Attn: _____   Client Industry: _____

Matter name: _____   Source of Client: _____

Description: _____   Referred by: _____

Practice Area   Thank you to referrer

RATES ☐ Pro Bono ☐ Flat Fee ☐ Contingency   Standard Hourly Rates: ☐ A ☐ B ☐ C ☐ D   ☐ Special (Describe): _____

Billing: ☐ Monthly ☐ Quarterly ☐ On Completion

DOCKET CONTROL		CONFLICT CONTROL	
Statute of Limitations		NAME	RELATIONSHIP
Tort Claims Act Notice Due			
First Appearance Due			
Other Deadlines			
File Review Frequency			
INSTRUCTIONS:			

Conflicts Entered by: _____

Conflicts Approved by: _____

Deadlines Docketed by: _____

Return file to: _____

File Opened by: _____

Sub Folders:
☐ Admin   ☐ Client Docs:
☐ Correspondence   ☐ Final Docs:
☐ Pleadings   ☐ Drafts
☐ Atty Notes/Memos   ☐ Title Report
☐ Legal Research   ☐ Loan Docs
☐ Bills:
☐ Other:_____

Physical file made by: _____

Appendix 3

Sample Disengagement Letter

(date)
Morrison and Charlotte Horner
Horner Family LLC
1234 Wiley Place
Somewhere, Oregon
Re: TransitCorp condemnation / conclusion of the project

Dear Mr. and Mrs. Horner:

   Now that we have concluded the litigation and settlement with TransitCorp with your transfer to TransitCorp of the property and payment to Horner Family LLC of the agreed sale price, we have completed the project for which you engaged us. I enclose our final invoice for our services and disbursements.

   This concludes our representation of Horner Family LLC in this matter, and I will close my file. It has been a pleasure to represent Horner Family LLC, and I appreciate the opportunity to have been of service and to have helped you reach this agreement with TransitCorp.

Very truly yours,
SAMPLE LAW FIRM LLP

Appendix 4

Recommended Additional Reading

How to Start and Build a Law Practice, Jay G. Foonberg, available
through the American Bar Association. Complete and
thorough, Mr. Foonberg's book covers everything you
need to know to open a small law office from scratch.
How to Draft Bills Clients Rush to Pay, J. Harris Morgan; second
edition by J. Harris Morgan and Jay G. Foonberg, published
by the Law Practice Management Section of the American Bar
Association. The authors explain how to use your invoices to tell
your clients not just what you did, but what you did for them.
Managing the Professional Service Firm, David H. Maister (1993),
published by Simon & Schuster. This book compiles 32 articles
that Professor Maister wrote on different aspects of managing
a professional service firm, with examples drawn from law,
accounting, and consulting to illustrate the author's advice on
business strategy, marketing services, and managing professionals.
Networking with the Affluent and Their Advisors, Thomas J.
Stanley (1993), published by Business One Irwin. Professor
Stanley has focused his academic career on studying
America's affluent. This is one of his three books on how to
meet and market to the affluent. It's oriented to sellers of
financial services but offers many tips and ideas that lawyers
can use. His star networker, in fact, is an accountant.
Selling Your Services, Robert W. Bly (1992), published in trade
paperback by Henry Holt and Company. The author, an

211

independent professional writer of sales letters, brochures, and marketing materials, lays out the basics for a solo operator to market his or her services. Fast, clear, readable.

The Checklist Manifesto, Atul Gawande (2009), published by Henry Holt and Company. The author, a surgeon, argues that failure in the modern world is more often the result of not using information that we know than the result of not knowing enough, and that many errors are errors of omission that the use of checklists would prevent.

Afterword

Even a book with the name of only one author on the cover is the result of the effort and experience of many. I gratefully appreciate the contributions of those whose ideas, support, and constructive criticism made it possible for me to write this book and for you to read it.

People I've never met have helped through their writing and ideas to shape this book, including Jay Foonberg, whose encyclopedic volume *How to Start and Build a Law Practice* established the standard for books on this topic; David Maister, whose research and writing on professional firms I studied in detail before I opened my own practice; and Thomas J. Stanley, who (before becoming widely known for his book *The Millionaire Next Door*) wrote the best book on networking that I have yet read, *Networking with the Affluent and Their Advisors*.

Lawyers have no monopoly on good ideas. My ideas on controlling the telephone are due in large part to Craig Cooley, the Oregon broker for whom I worked for eight years as a real estate agent. Other ideas in this book resulted from exchanges with Denise Tapp of Memphis, Tennessee, and her long experience in real estate.

One reason to attend seminars sponsored by the American Bar Association is to meet other lawyers in the same practice area. The idea for this book came about from a conversation with Michael J. Glazerman of the Massachusetts Bar at a seminar presented by the section of Real Property, Trust and Estate Law of the ABA. I hope Michael is pleased with the result.

Many people have ideas for books, but few of the ideas turn into books. That the idea became this book is due to the cajolery, persistence, patience, and gentle impatience first of Richard M. Frome of the New York Bar, who persuaded me to write and submit the outline of what I would put into this book, and then of Cynthia Boyer Blakeslee of the Pennsylvania Bar, who got me to actually write it. This book wouldn't exist without their efforts. I'm also appreciative of advice and comment from Cynthia, from Jeffrey

Salyards of the ABA, and especially from my wife, Susan T. Alterman of the Oregon Bar, and our son, Harrison Alterman, who took time away from his homework to read and comment on earlier drafts.

Finally, I owe a debt of gratitude to the late Raymond M. Kell and the late Clifford B. Alterman, longtime law partners in Portland, Oregon, who were the first to show me how to build a law practice. From a very early age, I watched as they built their two-lawyer firm into a 20-lawyer office, where with Mr. Kell's encouragement I started my legal career in 1989. Their ideas on marketing and building a practice appear in one form or another on nearly every page of this book. Mr. Kell was one of the finest legal writers I have ever known. I like to think that I've done justice to some of the principles of good writing that Mr. Kell taught me. I believe Dad would be proud of me also.

Index